D0916577

Praise for

Building Circles of Grace

"The tween years are often challenging for girls and their moms to navigate. Resources like *Building Circles of Grace* are a godsend for those of us who want to guide our girls to a deeper faith during these often tumultuous years. This Bible study for moms to do *with* their daughters is an opportunity to speak wisdom and truth into their hearts during a season when the world is telling them what they lack. *Circles of Grace* will help moms help their daughters build godly friendships, which is such an important part of adolescence. If you have a tween daughter, you need this Bible study!"

> **—Teri Lynne Underwood,** girl mom cheerleader, founder of Prayers for Girls, author of *Praying for Girls: Asking God for the Things They Need Most*, and proud mother of a beautiful inside-and-out daughter

"For Christian moms desiring intimate, meaty, and eternal connections with their tween daughters, *Building Circles of Grace* is a welcomed treasure. Catherine Bird seamlessly meshes timeless biblical truth with contemporary struggles of relationship, helping both generations embrace Christ's love for us and in us. I so wish a study like this had existed during my tween years; my mom and I would have relished drawing closer together as we also drew closer to the Father."

> **—Ava Sturgeon,** author of the teen Bible studies *A Daughter's Worth* and *A Daughter's Heart*

"Moms of young girls need a lot of tools to help their daughters reach their potential. *Building Circles of Grace* is one of those tools, helping a mom invest in her relationship with her girl and empowering a young girl to build her own best network of positive relationships in her life."

> **—Lynn Cowell,** speaker with Proverbs 31 Ministries and author of *Brave Beauty*

"As a mother of adult daughters, I can say that I wish I had this resource available to me when my girls were tweens. It's biblical, relatable, and an excellent follow-up to the first book in the series. The emphasis on relationships with practical wisdom and insights for navigating friendships in today's world will meet the real, felt needs of tweens . . . and the moms that love them."

> **—Anna LeBaron,** author of *The Polygamist's Daughter*

BUILDING circles of grace

a JOINT BIBLE STUDY
FOR TWEEN GIRLS aND THEIR MOMS

♥ CaTHERINE BIRD ♥

LEAFWOOD
PUBLISHERS
an imprint of Abilene Christian University Press

BUILDING CIRCLES OF GRACE

A Joint Bible Study for Tween Girls and Their Moms

LEAFWOOD
PUBLISHERS
an imprint of Abilene Christian University Press

Copyright © 2017 by Catherine Bird

ISBN 978-0-89112-453-5

Printed in the United States of America

ALL RIGHTS RESERVED
No part of this publication may be reproduced, stored in a retrieval system, or transmitted in any form by any means—electronic, mechanical, photocopying, recording, or otherwise—without prior written consent.

Scripture quotations noted *The Message* taken from *The Message*. Copyright © 1993, 1994, 1995, 1996, 2000, 2001, 2002. Used by permission of NavPress Publishing Group.

Scripture quotations noted NIV are from The Holy Bible, New International Version®, NIV®. Copyright © 1973, 1978, 1984, 2011 by Biblica, Inc.® Used by permission. All rights reserved worldwide.

Scripture quotations noted NLT are taken from the Holy Bible, New Living Translation, copyright ©1996, 2004, 2007, 2015 by Tyndale House Foundation. Used by permission of Tyndale House Publishers, Inc., Carol Stream, IL 60188. All rights reserved.

Scripture quotations noted ESV are from The ESV® Bible (The Holy Bible, English Standard Version®) copyright © 2001 by Crossway, a publishing ministry of Good News Publishers. ESV® Text Edition: 2011. The ESV® text has been reproduced in cooperation with and by permission of Good News Publishers. Unauthorized reproduction of this publication is prohibited. All rights reserved.

Scripture quotations marked NLV are taken from the NEW LIFE Version, © Christian Literature International.

Scripture quotations noted KJV are taken from the King James Version of the Bible.

Scripture quotations marked HCSB are taken from the Holman Christian Standard Bible®, Copyright © 1999, 2000, 2002, 2003, 2009 by Holman Bible Publishers. Used by permission. Holman Christian Standard Bible®, Holman CSB®, and HCSB® are federally registered trademarks of Holman Bible Publishers.

Scripture quotations noted NASB are taken from the New American Standard Bible® Copyright © 1960, 1962, 1963, 1968, 1971, 1972, 1973, 1975, 1977, 1995 by The Lockman Foundation. Used by permission.

Cover design by ThinkPen Design, LLC, and Strong Design

Leafwood Publishers is an imprint of Abilene Christian University Press
ACU Box 29138
Abilene, Texas 79699

1-877-816-4455
www.leafwoodpublishers.com

17 18 19 20 21 22 / 7 6 5 4 3 2 1

CONTENTS

Dedication

For my daughters, Ashley and Emma Kathryn.

You two girls and your daddy are absolutely the biggest and brightest blessings the Lord has ever gifted me. Not a day goes by that I am not incredibly thankful God made me your mama. The gift of family is your blessing, too, so always give thanks and cherish your sisterhood. As I watch you two grow and develop into the special girls of grace God designed you to be, I pray the Lord will surround you with wonderful friends who reinforce your identity as image bearers of Christ. True friends who will be there for you. Pray with you. Dream with you. Laugh with you. Celebrate or cry with you. Encourage and affirm you. Be accountable with you.

Friends love through all kinds of weather,
and families stick together in all kinds of trouble.

(Prov. 17:17 *The Message*)

acknowledgments

My husband is one amazing man, and the *Girls of Grace* Bible study series would not be a reality without his love and support. My Prince Charming has spent countless hours praying with me, praying over me, and praying for each of you who we hope will be touched in some way by these Bible studies.

Rev. Roland Timberlake, who married my husband and me, once sat with us in premarital counseling and said he knew we were in love. Yet we would not and could not understand how deeply we could love one another until we had traveled much of life's road together. We laughed at the time and wondered how we could ever love one another more than we already did. After nearly eighteen years of marriage, I am beginning to understand. This man God chose to be the other half of me has stood steadfast through the equally beautiful and arduous path of life and loved me through thick and thin—literally. Life is not always smooth, but it is always blessed. Thank you for loving me, honey. I love you *more.*

Thanks also to the moms and daughters who piloted the content of this study. I love Bible study class with my mamas and tween girls! Y'all make it so fun! Your friendships are sweet blessings that my daughters and I continue to cherish.

Long ago, God gifted me with my very best gal pal. We have journeyed through marriage and motherhood together, sometimes with laughter and sometimes with tears. Through fair skies and storms, this girl of grace has stood steadfast in her devotion and love for me. I have many dear friends whom I love more than words can convey, but she is truly the sister of my heart. Kathryn, I will always be thankful for the day God led me into your office at the Texas A&M College of Architecture! I heart you big time, sister.

My prayer warrior friends, who are too many to name—you know who you are. Thank you for your prayers and words of encouragement. And thank you for loving me even when I disappeared into my writing hole. I love you all.

introduction

This eight-week study is designed for tween girls (approximately ages nine to twelve) and their moms. The first study in this series, *Becoming a Girl of Grace*, examines the qualities and characteristics that the Bible's girls of grace demonstrate and how we can apply the lessons from their lives to ours today. Throughout *Becoming a Girl of Grace*, moms and tween girls explore what it means to have a personal relationship with God and what it means to be a girl of grace. *Building Circles of Grace* takes moms and daughters through the next step as they discuss what it means to build and sustain Christ-centered connections beyond their own relationship with Jesus.

Some of the toughest experiences we encounter as young girls (and moms, too) are a result of the people we choose as friends. How do you respond with grace to a bully? How do you cope with the loss of a friendship? Can you really make a difference by putting Jesus first when it's not the socially acceptable thing to do? And what exactly is a Christ-centered relationship? *Building Circles of Grace* addresses all of these questions and more.

Also, this study is intentionally written for tween girls to share with their moms. Tween girls may be surprised by their moms' perspectives, and moms may find a surprise or two as well! God made each and every one of us uniquely in his image. That means that while we are all created in his image, every single one of us is different and special in our own way. This includes moms and daughters. Moms have many talents, it's true! However, while she may have her daughter convinced she can read her mind, a mom does not necessarily know what is in her daughter's heart and mind unless her daughter expresses these thoughts and feelings. This study is a great way for moms and tween daughters to connect and share!

Format of the Study

This study is unique in that each chapter is not broken down into daily reading and study. This is an eight-week format designed to facilitate joint Bible study and discussion between moms and tween daughters. Moms and daughters may approach weekly study however it fits into their schedules. If you want to read and study a little bit each day, great! If it works better for you to consolidate into two days, go for it. The structure of this study is intentionally flexible.

There are a few ways to approach the Girls of Grace Heart Check sections within this study, which include conversation starters and questions to get you thinking more deeply about each chapter discussion. Answer the questions in each chapter together or on your own. Some moms and daughters may choose to write directly in the Bible study book, while others may prefer a notebook or journal where you can jot down your thoughts separately. My girls and I prefer the latter and also use our journals to keep our own prayer lists. Choose whatever method works best for you. If you are going through this study with a group, your facilitator will lead you through some engaging discussions and fun activities that relate to each week's topic.

Mom and Me Activities

In this study, you will also find activities specifically designed for moms and daughters to complete together each week. These activities are meant to facilitate fellowship between moms and daughters while helping them dig a little deeper into the biblical topic of each chapter. Have fun and feel free to include other family members. This can be an exciting adventure, so enjoy and get started today!

CHAPTER 1

CELEBRATING
THE BEAUTY OF YOU

So God created human beings in his own image.
In the image of God he created them;
male and female he created them.

(Gen. 1:27 NLT)

GIRLS OF GRACE, you are the image bearers of God. What this means is that human beings reflect God in a way that is unlike any other part of his creation. Although man was formed from the dust of the ground, God personally "breathed into his nostrils the breath of life; and man became a living being" (Gen. 2:7 NASB).

Just like we reflect certain genetic attributes of our earthly parents, God gifted his image bearers with certain likenesses unique to him. For example, our commonality with God is visible in our spiritual, mental, moral, and social characteristics. We know God does not have a body, although he has appeared to man (Gen. 18:1–2, 32:30; Exod. 33:11; Num. 14:14). Every human possesses a spirit, and thus we are more than the sum of our physical parts. Our spiritual nature, though unseen, is as real as our physical nature. We must feed our spirits just as we feed our bodies.

God also bestowed upon humans mental strength greater than any other living creature and gave man dominion over them (Gen. 1:26). This gift of intelligence has given us the ability to create art, compose music, count to large numbers, and compute complex mathematical equations (well, some of us). Our minds as designed by God give us the power to reason, to make decisions, to laugh, to dream.

We also have moral reasoning, which means God gave us the ability to tell right from wrong. Remember that Adam's and Eve's eyes were opened when they made a choice to disobey God and eat from the tree of the knowledge of good and evil (Gen. 3). As a result, they were forced to leave the garden and work *by the sweat of their faces* to eat bread (Gen. 3:19 NLV). With moral understanding comes accountability for our actions.

Lastly, God—who *is* love—created man with a social nature and a need for love. Eve was created as a helper for Adam so he would not be alone (Gen. 2:20–23). The statement in Genesis 3:8 (KJV) that "they heard the voice of the LORD God walking in the garden in the cool of the day" suggests that Adam and Eve enjoyed fellowship and communion with God, perhaps on a daily basis. We also see community in the Trinity, which is comprised of the Father, the Son, and the Holy Spirit. We were designed in the likeness of God as relational creatures to crave community.

So do you see? From the beginning, God set us apart. You were set apart *intentionally* with great love.

Loving the Person God Created You to Be

What do you see when you look in the mirror? Do you see a beautiful girl of grace who God created with love and care? Do you see inward beauty as well as outward attractiveness? Are you critical of yourself? What do you say to the reflection that stares back at you?

We live in a world and culture that puts much effort into telling girls (small and tall) what we should think is beautiful. Think about the images of girls and women you see every day. Do not just think about the commercials and female celebrities that our eyes take in from day to day, but also think about the girls you encounter in public places, at school, at church, and everywhere else in your daily life. These outward images have a profound impact on how we see ourselves, and we often let these images set the standard for our own ideals of beauty. How dangerous is that?

> *Before I formed you in the womb I knew you,*
> *before you were born I set you apart;*
> *I appointed you as a prophet to the nations.*
>
> Jer. 1:5 (NIV)

God's idea of beauty is not defined by the latest trends or who is most popular at school. God *created* beauty! The beauty of the earth and everything in it (including you) was designed and defined by God. The verse from Jeremiah reminds us that God designed each and every one of us in our mothers' wombs. Even though we are created in the image of God, he also formed each and every person in a unique and special way. There is no other individual like you, and God did that on purpose! You are beautiful, and God is proud of his creation in you. That is the standard by which we should set our idea of what it means to be beautiful.

Sometimes, though, we think beauty refers only to an outwardly pleasing appearance. However, beauty encompasses all of you—your body, mind, and spirit—which God knitted with perfect care and detail. *Merriam-Webster* defines beauty this way: "the quality or aggregate of qualities in a person or thing that gives pleasure to the senses or pleasurably exalts the mind or spirit: loveliness."

Every hair, every bone—all of you down to the core of your spirit is exactly how God designed you to be. I know. I know. When you are sitting in class, and the most popular girl in school has made fun of you—again—it is tough to remember that what she thinks is fleeting and inconsequential. Or perhaps you have hurt someone else by allowing that person to believe he or she is ugly, unworthy, and unimportant. How do we break this cycle and retrain our brains and hearts to see others and ourselves as God designed us to be?

The answer is in the Word God has given us. The most important thing we are asked to remember is this:

> *"Teacher, which is the greatest commandment in the Law?"*
>
> *Jesus replied: "'Love the Lord your God with all your heart and with all your soul and with all your mind.' This is the first and greatest commandment. And the second is like it: 'Love your neighbor as yourself.' All the Law and the Prophets hang on these two commandments."*
>
> Matt. 22:36–40 (NIV)

This study is about learning how to build and sustain Christ-centered relationships within your circle of people (what I will call your circle of grace—because you are God's girl of grace!). Your circle is broader than your circle of friends and encompasses both relationships you choose for yourself and relationships you did not necessarily pick on your own. For example, you choose your friends. Those relationships are completely voluntary (which we will talk about in more depth in Chapter Three). Other relationships reflect connections that you may not have selected for yourself. This may include your parents (and other family members), a teacher, a pastor, or perhaps your teammates. This is by no means an exclusive list, and you will get the idea of how your circles are formed and who they include in Chapter Two.

You are at the heart of your circle, and God is at the heart of you. Look back at Matthew 22:36–38. First and foremost, Jesus wants to be your BFF. He longs for a relationship with you. The time that you spend talking, texting, and laughing with your gal pals is the kind of carefree transparency that God longs to have with you. The bottom line, girls, is that we need God. He created us. He loves us. He should be at the heart of everything we do, because he is at the heart of us.

What exactly do we mean when we speak of Christ-centered relationships? When we establish connections with other people, we are sharing a piece of ourselves, right? You are giving these individuals a little glimpse inside your heart to see what makes you who you are. If you are at the heart of your circle and God is at the heart of you, he will be reflected in your relationships with other people. When we talk about Christ-centered relationships, we mean keeping Jesus smack-dab in the middle of your connections with everyone, whether they are family members, close friends, or distant acquaintances. Keeping Christ at the center of your circle means his light shines through you every single day in every single encounter you have with the people in your life.

Do not let this scare you, girls. You may think, "Oh, no! I can never mess up!" That is simply not true. We will mess up and often. God knows we are not perfect. That is why he sent his one and only Son to save us. God longs for us to keep him as close as he keeps us, so that when we do make a mistake, we feel his grace, mercy, and love.

 ## girl of grace HearT CHECK

♥ What do you think it means to be beautiful? What does Mom think? Are your definitions similar or different?

♥ Did your definition of beauty include inward beauty (of heart and mind) as well as physical appearance? Talk with Mom about why or why not.

♥ Read 1 Peter 3:3—4 and write it out in the space below.

♥ What does Peter mean about unfading beauty and how does that relate to one's worthiness?

♥ Do you think you are beautiful in God's eyes? How do you think God sees you?

♥ Mom, how about you? Do you agree with what God sees when you look in the mirror?

♥ Write below what you think it means to have a Christ-centered relationship.

an activity for mom and me: rECOGNIZING BeAUTIFUL

- ♥ Start with four pieces of drawing paper—two for Mom and two for you.
- ♥ You will also need drawing pencils (regular pencils will work) or colored pencils.
- ♥ Using your bathroom mirror or another mirror (standing makeup mirrors work great), both mom and daughter should draw their self-portraits. Do not show one another your work! If you need to use separate mirrors so you are not tempted to look, then do it.
- ♥ Set aside your self-portrait when it is complete (being careful not to show one another your work just yet), and grab the remaining two sheets of drawing paper.
- ♥ Mom and daughter, now take turns drawing a portrait of the other.
- ♥ When you have finished both pictures, set the portraits side by side to compare.

How are the pictures different? How are they similar? Sometimes we have a difficult time seeing the beauty that God and others see in us. Talk with mom about the beauty you see in one another and what being beautiful means to you. You may be delightfully surprised by what you hear!

The Holy Spirit Dwells Within You

As girls, we tend to be very critical of ourselves. It is tough not to compare your hair, your body, and the qualities that make you who you are with other girls. Why do we do this? Well, because we are human—and because we are girls!

In addition to being a girl, being a tween girl can be especially scary. Your body is changing. Sometimes you are sad or feel like crying—but you are not sure why. You may be through losing baby teeth and headed toward braces (if you are not already there). You are no longer a little girl, but you still have a bit of growing to do before you become a teenager. You are literally in beTWEEN one phase and another. There is lot going on with your body, your mind, and your spirit. Sometimes you feel awkward with all these changes.

I remember going through a particularly painful growth spurt in the fifth grade. I felt clumsy and unwieldy. At my school, the fifth grade lockers were in a breezeway next to all the classrooms. When we changed subjects (which sometimes meant changing teachers), all the fifth graders would cram together in this little area in a hurry to swap books for the next class. One day, I was walking to my locker during a class transition, and my legs got away from me. I do not know what happened! One second, I was walking toward my locker with all my books. Then, the next thing I knew, I was flat on my tummy with my books scattered in all directions. My fifth grade friends pointed and laughed, and I was humiliated!

This was the first time I remember thinking, "I don't feel like me." I did not feel beautiful and specially crafted by God. You know what? I can also remember awful experiences like the one I had in the locker room happening to my other friends. The truth was we were all changing and growing. No one was immune to the spirit of clumsiness or embarrassment.

Moms go through changes like this, too. Believe it or not, girls, moms feel awkward and out of place sometimes just like you. Change is tough—especially when those changes are happening inside you and to your own body.

The constant through all these changes is God. Who better to lean on than the One who crafted and created you? No matter what is happening in your life, God is the one friend you can always count on to stick with you through thick and through thin. Of course, there will be others who love and support you (like your family and friends), but no one will ever know you like God does. And you know what? He loves everything about you! As much as your mama may love and adore you, even she cannot count the number of hairs on your head—but God can! "And the very hairs on your head are all numbered" (Luke 12:7 NLT).

God does not make mistakes, and he thinks all of his creations are beautiful. That includes you, Miss Girl of Grace! The Bible is full of marvelous examples of God's love for us, like this passage: "I praise you because I am fearfully and wonderfully made; your works are wonderful, I know that full well" (Ps. 139:14 NIV). Never doubt your beauty—of your body, mind, or spirit. This does not mean you will not doubt yourself occasionally. Just remember the next time you see someone you think is beautiful, ask yourself if you are measuring by society's standard or by God's.

Celebrate the beauty in yourself. You are fearfully and wonderfully made! I am going to repeat myself. At the heart of your circle is *you*. At the heart of you is God. Your relationship with God is the foundation for your own circle of grace. If you keep Christ at the center of your heart, you are laying a solid foundation for Christ-centered relationships with others.

 girl of grace HearT CHECK

♥ Can you think of a time when you have felt unbeautiful? What circumstances led you to feel this way? How did you overcome this feeling? Mom, you share, too.

♥ Read Matthew 22:36–40 and write it below.

♥ Are you following these commandments? Talk with mom about why or why not.

♥ If you are having trouble living into God's instruction to love your neighbor, brainstorm with mom about ways to overcome any obstacles in your path. Pray together and ask God to remove these roadblocks and give you a heart to love others as he does.

♥ Discuss with mom what it means to love yourself.

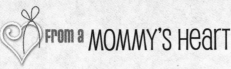

From a MOMMY'S HEart

As I was mourning the loss of my baby girl's toddler phase—especially knowing my husband and I would not have another baby—a very dear friend gave me some wonderful advice. She encouraged me to mourn the passing of each phase, but she also cautioned me not to miss an opportunity to celebrate the wonderful experiences we would encounter with each new phase of our children's development. She was so right!

My youngest darling did not sleep through the night until she was three and a half years old. Being sleep-deprived with a new baby was one thing. Getting caught with your pants on inside out and backwards when your baby is three is mortifying! And yes. This really happened. Thankfully, it was my BFF who happened to notice, and I had yet to leave the house that day.

Early motherhood was about survival. I am convinced this is why we took tons and tons of pictures. We were so tired! Looking back now, we often say. "Oh, I forgot about that!" I loved having wee baby girls, and sometimes I do miss those tiny feet and gently lulling my little ones to sleep.

These days, however, we are less about sleep schedules and more about school and extracurricular activities. The older my girls get, the more mileage I put on my car. I would not trade it, though. My dear friend was right. There is something new and amazing with each phase of development. The tween years are no different.

My tween girl's friends are definitely important to her, but she still treasures our mommy/daughter time. In a world that encourages our kiddos to grow up much faster than they should, I'm a-okay with the big girl kisses and snuggles. Her heart is still open to the mommy wisdom I wish to impart, and I am thankful. She still absorbs so much—as children are prone to do—but now I am even more aware of how my actions are influencing how she feels about herself. Now, please do not misunderstand.

My husband and I love and adore our daughters, and we take every opportunity to tell and show them how important and special they are in God's kingdom.

I am talking about the self-deprecating comments I mutter under my breath about myself. No, I am not the weight I was in college. I have had two babies, and things are arranged a little differently now. Even as I warn my tween darling to beware of society's definition of beautiful, I am just as vulnerable to the assault on my self-confidence. My daughter watches how I deal with the days I do not feel beautiful, and I have heard her make similar comments about herself.

Moms, this is our chance to be real with our girls. I have never claimed to be perfect—far from it. I am a girl of grace in training just like everyone else. My sweet husband has loved me through thick and thin—literally. Sometimes I am self-conscious about my body, and he shakes his head and adamantly reminds me how beautiful I am to him.

That is a need God can fulfill for us! I fall prey to the ill-defined worldly view of beauty from time to time, but I have also found myself talking with my tween daughter about how these insecurities are a fallacy that Satan uses to distract us. We were created out of love, for love. We are all beautiful in the eyes of God, and it is nice to remind one another _and_ ourselves of this on the days when we feel any less than the lovely girls of grace God created us to be!

CHAPTER 2

BUILDING CIRCLES OF GRACE—
WHERE DOES YOUR CIRCLE BEGIN?

"This is My command:
Love one another as I have loved you."

(John 15:12 HCSB)

YOU UNDERSTAND FROM CHAPTER ONE that you are God's image bearer, and as such, you share attributes with our Creator. One such characteristic is the need for community. Connectivity with other human beings is something each of us craves. No matter how God designed you—extrovert, introvert, socially skilled, or socially awkward—something in your spirit longs for meaningful relationships with other humans.

The Holy Trinity beautifully models perfect community for us. The Nicene Creed (c. AD 325) is one of the oldest and most cherished church doctrines (which simply means this is a belief the church holds true). It summarizes the Trinity this way:

> *We believe in one God, the Father, the Almighty, maker*
> *of heaven and earth, of all that is, seen and unseen. We*
> *believe in one Lord, Jesus Christ, the only Son of God,*
> *eternally begotten of the Father, God from God, Light*
> *from Light, true God from true God, begotten, not made,*
> *of one Being with the Father. Through him all things*
> *were made. . . . We believe in the Holy Spirit, the Lord,*
> *the giver of life, who proceeds from the Father and the*
> *Son. With the Father and the Son he is worshiped and*
> *glorified. He has spoken through the Prophets.*

We discussed briefly that the Trinity means God himself is in community. More accurately, God *is* community: one God, three persons. Before any sort of human community existed, there was God, dwelling in perfect, loving harmony in his three-person being.

Genesis 1:26 says, "Let *us* make mankind in our image" (NIV, emphasis mine). Human beings are made in the image of God to reflect his likeness. This is why our longing for community feels so deeply rooted. We are hard-wired as God's image bearers to crave connectivity. Community also does not simply mean close physical proximity. Rather, we long to connect with others through deep, meaningful relationships.

It is through these relationships with others that God blesses us with a place to be loved, a place to be accountable, a place to pray and worship, a place to serve, a place to witness. God's Word is *rich* with instruction on how we should build and sustain community. We will dig deeper in this chapter and unpack what the Bible has to say about this. Let's get started!

Understanding relationships

As we dig deeper into the heart of this study, you now understand your circle of grace begins with you and God. You are at the heart of your circle, and God is at the heart of you. To this foundation, you will add other relationships and connections to your circle. Remember, your circle reflects the people (or relationships) who surround you in life—whether by choice or circumstance. So what is a relationship? According to *The Free Dictionary*, a relationship is "a particular type of connection existing between people related to or having dealings with each other."

The relationship between you and your parents is familial, which merely means you are part of the same family. Any family member—siblings, grand-parents, aunts, uncles, cousins, and so on—will fall into this category. These are relationships that God selects for you (adopted and blended families included). Growing up, I know sometimes my brothers and I wished we had a choice when picking our siblings! Eventually, though, we realized how great God's plan was to put us together. God does not make mistakes, so his plan to place you where you are was done with a loving purpose—even if sometimes it does not feel like it.

The Bible is full of examples of familial relationships, but let us look specifically at the relationship between Ruth and Naomi. Take a moment to read Ruth 1:1–18. This passage explains to us the type of familial relationship that these two women had. Ruth was married to Naomi's son. When he died, custom would have dictated that Ruth return to her father's house. That is not what happened, though. Look again at verses 16–18:

> *But Ruth replied, "Don't urge me to leave you or to turn back from you. Where you go I will go, and where you stay I will stay. Your people will be my people and your God my God. Where you die I will die, and there I will be buried. May the LORD deal with me, be it ever so severely, if even death separates you and me." When Naomi realized that Ruth was determined to go with her, she stopped urging her. (NIV)*

Ruth's relationship with Naomi was inherited—meaning Ruth was connected to Naomi through her marriage to Naomi's son. We all know relationships with family members are not always easy. We disagree, and sometimes we wonder how we are related to such strange individuals. I often thought this with my brothers!

God does understand the reason for our family connections, though. Naomi experienced incredible loss in a short period of time in her life—losing her husband and both of her sons. Can you imagine how sad she was? God connected Ruth to Naomi's family, and the two women developed a great devotion and trust for one another. Think how much Ruth must have loved and respected her mother-in-law to leave the only home she had ever known to live in a country she had never seen! The love, devotion, and trust these two women had for one another resulted in a deep and lasting friendship.

My brothers and I disagreed daily when we were kids. It did not matter who started the argument, eye rolling and finger pointing seemed to be a daily event. However, my brothers were extremely territorial. Apparently, only they could pick on me. I learned to depend on them. Even though we disagreed—and often—I knew when the going got tough, my brothers would be there for me. Today, we laugh and enjoy a friendship we did not have as kids. Now there is hardly any eye rolling and finger pointing at all!

Do not miss out on the blessings of these neat people just because you did not get a choice in picking your familial connections! Remember, the Creator placed you where you are, and he did so with a loving and specific purpose. These relationships can be some of the biggest, brightest blessings in your circle of grace.

There are other relationships in your life that you do not necessarily pick for yourself. These connections may include your teacher, your dentist, your pastor, and perhaps classmates at school. Even though you may not be best buds with a classmate or teammate, these individuals are still peripherally part of your circle. You still have to interact with them, and sometimes God uses these connections in a big way.

Let me give you an example. Jesus's twelve disciples were an unlikely group of friends. They did not have a whole lot in common when God brought them together. In a sense, these men were classmates, and their teacher was Jesus! To be a disciple means to be a student or learner of a particular teacher or person. Think about your class at school or your Sunday school group. Sometimes, you may think the only thing you have in common is having the same teacher. God took a group of men from different professions, different families, and different places in life and brought them together for really important work.

> *One day as Jesus was preaching on the shore of the Sea of Galilee, great crowds pressed in on him to listen to the word of God. He noticed two empty boats at the water's edge, for the fishermen had left them and were washing their nets. Stepping into one of the boats, Jesus asked Simon, its owner, to push it out into the water. So he sat in the boat and taught the crowds from there.*
>
> *When he had finished speaking, he said to Simon, "Now go out where it is deeper, and let down your nets to catch some fish."*
>
> *"Master," Simon replied, "we worked hard all last night and didn't catch a thing. But if you say so, I'll let the nets down again." And this time their nets were so full of fish they began to tear! A shout for help brought their partners in the other boat, and soon both boats were filled with fish and on the verge of sinking.*
>
> *When Simon Peter realized what had happened, he fell to his knees before Jesus and said, "Oh, Lord, please leave me—I'm such a sinful man." For he was awestruck by the number of fish they had caught, as were the others with him. His partners, James and John, the sons of Zebedee, were also amazed.*

Jesus replied to Simon, "Don't be afraid! From now on you'll be fishing for people!" And as soon as they landed, they left everything and followed Jesus.

Luke 5:1–11 NLT

God places people in our lives, just as he places us in the paths of others. Be open to these kinds of connections when you feel the Holy Spirit drawing you toward an unlikely friendship!

 girl of grace HearT CHeCK

♥ Look up the following passages and compare them. Talk with one another about how God is *one* God, and yet he exists in *three* persons.

▸ Genesis 1:1—

▸ John 1:1–4—

▸ Matthew 28:19—

▸ Deuteronomy 6:4—

♥ How does the Trinity impact your understanding of community?

♥ Family connections are important to your circle of grace. Can you list three reasons you are glad God placed your family together? Mom, you share, too!

  ▶

  ▶

  ▶

♥ Can you think of a time you made a good friend in an unlikely place or circumstance? What happened? Mom, what about you?

♥ Pray with Mom and ask God to open your heart to relationships that will allow him to transform you. Ask him to give you the wisdom and courage to acknowledge an opportunity for friendship with someone you may have thought was an unlikely companion.

MOM aND DauGHTer sLeePOVer!

This activity is just what it sounds like. I do not know any girl—small or tall—who does not love girls' night! Moms and daughters have one very important thing in common—we are girls! This Mom and Me activity is all about giggling, girl talk, and having fun. We love family night, but this is for girls only! Try to make arrangements for this sleepover party to be just moms and daughters.

Here are a few suggestions to get you started:

- ♥ Movies? Yes!
- ♥ Pizza? Yummy!
- ♥ Popcorn? Definitely!
- ♥ Nail painting? Hello! It's girls' night!! Of course!
- ♥ Games? Absolutely!
- ♥ Pajamas? Required attire!

A mom's connection with her daughter is something special. Boys are special, too! But this is about moms and daughters. This sleepover is a fun opportunity to connect and share. You can make this is as simple or elaborate as you like! If pennies permit, you may think about renting a hotel room and adding dinner at a restaurant beforehand. This activity is flexible and can be adjusted to fit any budget, so please do not let financial constraints keep you from setting aside this time together. The important thing is to carve out an evening of girl fun just for mom and daughter. You will have so much fun that this might become a regular date night!

instantly connected

What about the relationships you pick for yourself? Well, of course these individuals are extremely important to your circle of grace! These people are your friends and confidantes. Relationships with these folks are completely optional. You get to choose how much time you spend together and what to share of yourself.

Have you ever met someone and instantly felt a connection with him or her? Maybe it felt like you had known that person for a long time. You felt immediately comfortable in one another's company. Sometimes you meet a special someone and know instantly that you are supposed to be friends. It happens! Just look at the example of David and Jonathan shared with us in 1 Samuel.

> *After David had finished talking with Saul, he met Jonathan, the king's son. There was an immediate bond between them, for Jonathan loved David. From that day on Saul kept David with him and wouldn't let him return home. And Jonathan made a solemn pact with David, because he loved him as he loved himself. Jonathan sealed the pact by taking off his robe and giving it to David, together with his tunic, sword, bow, and belt.*
>
> 1 Sam. 18:1–4 NLT

It was a powerful demonstration of friendship when Jonathan gave his robe, tunic, sword, bow, and belt to David. He did not just offer him a friendly handshake. He offered David everything that reflected his own station of life. You may have heard the phrase, "I'd give you the shirt off my back." In the time of David and Jonathan, though, Jonathan's actions in this passage were a significant gesture!

David was a shepherd boy, and Jonathan was the prince of Israel. They probably did not have the same circle of friends. If you look a little earlier in 1 Samuel 17, you will see David was unaccustomed to the privileges afforded the king's family. When Saul offered his own armor for David to wear as he fought Goliath, David was discomforted by the unfamiliar equipment and declined to wear it into battle.

The point is it did not matter that David and Jonathan were from two very different backgrounds. They saw something inside one another that sparked a special friendship. The Bible tells us the connection between these two men was instantaneous, deep, and long lasting. These two would weather many storms together, but their friendship would stand the test of time.

> *And as soon as the boy had gone, David rose from beside the stone heap and fell on his face to the ground and bowed three times. And they kissed one another and wept with one another, David weeping the most.*
>
> 1 Sam. 20:41 ESV

This type of friendship is rare. Friendships like this are special, because they do not happen every day. These are the relationships in which we tend to invest a lot of ourselves, because we *chose* to be connected. We want to spend time with friends who allow us to feel like we can be ourselves and truly enjoy one another's company.

Not all of your friendships will be as deep and meaningful as the example modeled for us by David and Jonathan, and that is okay. That does not mean God will not use these relationships to bless you and your circle of grace!

Choose Wisely

We allow our friends to see parts of ourselves that we would not show to just anyone. Anytime we share a part of ourselves, we show vulnerability or openness. Anytime you open your heart, there is the risk that you will get hurt. This may have already happened to you.

This is why it is so important to choose our friends carefully. Do not mistake the message here, girls. Loving your neighbor as God calls us to do does not mean you will share the innermost part of your heart with every person you meet. Should you have that transparency with God? Absolutely! He already knows what is in your heart, but he wants you to tell him. God is the only friend you have with a direct and completely open line to your spirit. He created you. That is a friendship you can always trust.

Other friendships, though, are typically built over time—as you develop love, respect, and trust for one another. Sometimes people make mistakes and are not as careful and honorable with their friends' trust as they should be. It happens to all us at one point or another—whether intentional or not. When a trust is broken, it hurts. We will really dig into this topic in Chapter Three, but the lesson here is to ask God to help us choose our friends wisely.

Have you ever heard the song, "O, Be Careful Little Eyes"? It is an old children's Bible tune that you may remember from your younger days in Sunday school. Take a minute to look up the lyrics online and write them in the space below. Type into your search engine "O, Be Careful Little Eyes lyrics," and they should pop right up.

As simple and childlike as this song may be, it is a really great road map for building not only our relationship with God but also Christ-centered relationships with others. This sweet tune tells everything we need to know about how to build our own circle of grace.

Once your eyes take in a vision, that something cannot be *un*-seen. A message taken in by your ears is carried straight to your heart. As much as we might like to say, "Oh, I will make myself forget," that simply is not the way our human minds work. Have you ever seen a TV program or movie that you could not stop thinking about long after it was over? I still remember a scary movie I saw at a friend's house when I was in elementary school. We thought we were so grown up to be watching *Gremlins*. This movie still gives me chills, and I did not sleep for weeks after I saw it.

I am talking about more than TV shows, movies, and computer games, though. What about when someone whispers a secret in your ear about another friend or person you know? What about when you watch a kid sitting alone at lunch or being bullied by another group of kids? Our hearts and minds are susceptible to ugly thoughts and messages just as they crave affirming ones. Be careful little eyes what you see. Be careful little ears what you hear. Guard your hearts and minds, and ask God to help you choose your companions wisely.

 girl of grace HearT CHeck

♥ Talk with Mom about what the words to "O, Be Careful Little Eyes" mean to you. How are these lyrics a helpful reminder as we choose friends?

♥ Is there something you have seen or heard that is weighing on your heart? Talk with Mom and ask her to pray with you. Ask God to take this burden from your heart and replace it with encouraging words to share instead.

♥ Think about a time when someone you thought was a friend betrayed your trust. What happened?

♥ How did you handle the situation? Were you able to resolve the conflict and forgive? Mom, what about you?

♥ What qualities do you think are important in a friend? Why are these qualities important to you?

♥ Does your circle of friends share these qualities? Do you see these qualities in yourself?

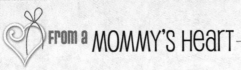
My mother's words float around in my head often as I search for the right way to talk with my girls about the importance of healthy friendships. Usually, this happens when my girls' feelings are hurt or they're angry as a result of a disagreement with one of their friends—and I find myself trying to find the right words to comfort, encourage, and counsel them.

When my babies were younger, my husband and I taught them the importance of getting along with others, sharing their toys, and using their words instead of hands or teeth to express how they felt when someone made them angry or hurt their feelings. We encouraged them to include all their friends and not to leave anyone out of whatever game they were playing. We would say, "Make good choices!"

We always have a choice. God is big on free will. I will readily admit my sweet husband and I do not always institute the whole "free will" concept as well with our children, but we try.

Choosing friends is one of the earliest opportunities for independence that we give our kids. I can remember my own parents telling me to choose my friends wisely, as those relationships could directly impact my emotional and spiritual health. Now, my tween darling may not grasp that concept fully, but she knows there is a voice inside her spirit that helps guide her decision-making.

Our children's friendships are sensitive territory. Some parents have really strong feelings about this topic. The best we can do is help our children understand the importance of choosing friends wisely. Will they make mistakes? Sure! I know I have made plenty. Some of the most painful life experiences I have personally lived through were a result of friendships that I chose. My choice of friends has also resulted in some of God's greatest blessings in my life.

It pains me to say it! I remember thinking my parents could not possibly understand how I felt when I was about to start middle school. I wanted to trust my parents' advice, but I was not sure they could really relate to what was happening between my friends and me. They were so old! (I am sorry, Mom!) Yes, times have changed. Blah! Blah! Blah! Mean girls are not a new phenomenon. BFFs have been around since the beginning of time. Hairstyles and clothing trends may change, but interpersonal relationships still work the same. (Sigh.) Mom, you were right.

My girls have heard their dad and me say on numerous occasions that friendships should be chosen with care. We also try reinforcing with our girls the importance of Christ-centered relationships with their friends. God is not someone you check at the door—ever. He is always with us. The only way I know how to stress the importance of Christ as the foundation of our relationships is to model through my own friendships as best as I can.

One of my best friends is Jewish. When I think of Christ-centered relationships, my relationship with this friend comes to mind. I love her so much that it is tough to convey with words. She does not believe that Jesus is God's one and only Son. She does not believe that God gave his one and only Son so that we could have a personal relationship with him and live with him forever. Does this stop me from loving her and being her friend? Absolutely not. God created her with the same love and purpose that he used to create the rest of us. She is a child of God, a daughter of the King, and my job is not to judge her. My job is to love her.

Jesus is at the center of my heart, so for me, he is also at the center of our friendship. I pray for her. I tell her that I pray for her. I am completely transparent with her just as she is with me. She knows what I believe and why I believe it. She even volunteers at the mom and daughter Christian retreats where I speak. When I look at her, I see this amazing individual specially crafted and designed with loving hands by a loving God. I would lay down my robe, tunic, sword, bow, and belt for my friend. I hope my girls are taking notice and trusting God to guide them as they choose which friendships to invest their hearts into.

CHAPTER 3

You've got
a FrieND IN Me

The arrow and the song

I shot an arrow into the air,
It fell to earth, I knew not where;
For, so swiftly it flew, the sight
Could not follow it in its flight.

I breathed a song into the air,
It fell to earth, I knew not where;
For who has sight so keen and strong,
That it can follow the flight of song?

Long, long afterward, in an oak
I found the arrow, still unbroke;
And the song, from beginning to end,
I found again in the heart of a friend.

.Henry Wadsworth Longfellow

Did you know that there are over 170,000 words in the English language, and roughly a quarter of these words are adjectives or what we call describing words? It is true! The Inuit people have nearly eighty different words for snow. Hawaiians have sixty-five words for describing fishing nets. While the English language is not *quite* as innovative, it still affords us with vast opportunities to differentiate meaning. For example, look at love and friendship.

What the English language lacks in synonyms (or words that are similar in meaning), it makes up for with the use of adjectives. *Close* friend. *Best* friend. *Childhood* friend. *Intimate* friend. *Trusted* friend. *Beloved* friend. With the different combinations of describing words, we could have vast meanings for such a simple word.

Friends are special people. We cannot pick our family. We have already established that God chooses our familial relationships. However, we can choose our friends, and these individuals can be as diverse and infinite as the adjectives we choose to describe them.

What Does Friendship mean to me?

Now we know who makes up your circle of grace. You know your circle is filled with both relationships you inherit and relationships you choose. Let us talk more about the connections you make for yourself. Remember, we call these types of people our friends. In the words of *Merriam Webster*, a friend is "a favored companion."

I love this definition! A favored companion is someone with whom we want to spend our time. If we took away the adjective "favored," a companion would simply be someone we spend time with. Think of all the people you spend time with on a daily basis. Perhaps you are at school or (for Mom) work. Spending time with a person does not necessarily make him or her your friend. A *favored* companion is so much more than that! We enjoy their companionship. Maybe we even crave their companionship. God created us out of love, for love, and he created us for community. He designed us for *favored* companionship. Look at what the Bible says in Ecclesiastes 4.

> *Two people are better off than one, for they can help each other succeed. If one person falls, the other can reach out and help. But someone who falls alone is in real trouble. Likewise, two people lying close together can keep each other warm. But how can one be warm alone? A person standing alone can be attacked and defeated, but two can stand back-to-back and conquer. Three are even better, for a triple-braided cord is not easily broken.*
>
> Eccles. 4:9–12 NLT

Friends play an important part in each of our lives, and friendships can make us stronger. A friend can make a really bad day seem not so gloomy or a really funny moment even funnier. When something really great happens to you, who are the first people you want to tell (besides your family)? Your friends! They celebrate your successes, and they mourn with you when you are sad. You do the same for them. This is the foundation of a positive friendship.

The Bible gives us several really great examples of friendship. Do you remember Abraham? He had a really good friend named Lot, who also happened to be his nephew. Abraham loved Lot. In the Book of Genesis, we learn that Lot was taken against his will. When Abraham learned something terrible had happened to his friend, he immediately took action to help him.

> *A fugitive came and reported to Abram the Hebrew.*
> *Abram was living at the Oaks of Mamre the Amorite,*
> *brother of Eshcol and Aner. They were allies of Abram.*
> *When Abram heard that his nephew had been taken*
> *prisoner, he lined up his servants, all of them born in his*
> *household—there were 318 of them—and chased after*
> *the captors all the way to Dan. Abram and his men split*
> *into small groups and attacked by night. They chased*
> *them as far as Hobah, just north of Damascus. They*
> *recovered all the plunder along with nephew Lot and his*
> *possessions, including the women and the people.*
>
> Gen. 14:14–16 *The Message*

This is what friends do! We stand up for one another. When I was in the fifth grade, another girl in my class passed a mean note about me to other classmates. It was hurtful, and I felt helpless to stand up to her actions alone. I do not even remember what the note said, but I do remember it contained an ugly message meant to hurt and embarrass me.

One of my best friends intercepted the note during class and threw it in the trash. When the author of the mean note continued saying ugly things on the playground, my friends stood with me to tell her the way she was acting was inappropriate and "uncool." My friends stood with me, and she stopped picking on me. I felt so thankful that my friends helped me stand up for myself.

What happened to me in the fifth grade happens to other people every day. It can happen to anyone—no matter how old we get. Yes, girls! Moms still encounter hurtful situations like this as adults. Sometimes, people make a poor choice to tear someone down instead of building her up as God calls us to do. How we react to situations like this helps define the kind of friend we are. Other people's actions are a reflection of their hearts. How you respond is a reflection of yours.

Have you ever heard of a fair-weather friend? This is a term for friends who only act like friends when skies are blue and all is right and well in the world. A fair-weather friend may not have stood with me against a bully if she cared more about what the bully thought of her than what she thought of our friendship. It is easy to be friends when there is no conflict, and everyone is happy. What happens when two friends from your circle have a disagreement? Or what happens when a friend of yours experiences pain and loss in some way? How do you normally respond?

True friendships stand the test of time and conflict. I have friends I do not see for years at a time. When we see one another or talk on the phone, we pick right up where we left off. That is not to say that friendships will not change and grow as we do. They absolutely will. Some friends are brought into our lives just for a season. Perhaps there is no great parting conflict; you simply grow apart. It happens. Whether you are building a long-lasting, lifetime friendship or traveling down a short stretch of life's long road together, you can be assured that God will not waste any experience or relationship in your life. They all have a purpose.

 girl of grace HearT CHecK

♥ Who are your favored companions? Mom, you answer, too!

♥ List at least three reasons you consider these pals with favor. What makes them special to you?

♥ Take turns sharing a time when your friends helped you feel strong in a situation that would have been tough to experience alone.

an activity for mom and me: SHOW ME THE WAY!

This week's activity is about doing something nice for a neighbor. For this activity, a neighbor does not necessarily mean the person who lives next door to you. You are going to live out Galatians 5:14! "For the entire law is fulfilled in keeping this one command: 'Love your neighbor as yourself'" (NIV).

Brainstorm with mom who you want to shower with an act of kindness this week. It can be an elderly neighbor on your street, a friend who needs help finding her smile, or anyone else you want to serve in a kind way. Here are a few ideas you may try:

- ♥ Take dinner to a sick friend.
- ♥ Bake cookies or another fun something and take it to a nursing home near where you live.
- ♥ Write a note to your pastor, teacher, or another leader who has positively impacted you.
- ♥ Invite a friend who needs a smile over for an old-fashioned tea party or sleepover.

Life is busy, and we do not always have time (or take the time) to actively show our neighbors that they are special in our eyes as well as God's. Whatever you decide to do and whoever you decide to shower with kindness this week, be sure to pass along the message in Galatians 5:14.

rough seas!

Some of the biggest and brightest blessings that God gives us in life come in the form of friends. Just like any blessing from God, we should treasure these gifts and treat them with care.

When you do not take care of something important to you, it tarnishes and falls into disrepair. For example, let us say you leave your favorite pair of roller skates outside and neglect to put them in your closet when you are not wearing them. It rains, then it is hot—Texas hot! They eventually break and get thrown away. Friendships can be like this, too!

You and a friend have likely had a disagreement at one time or another. Did it take both of you to resolve your differences and smooth the anger or hurt you felt? Likely, one of you (or both) apologized, both sides forgave, and you moved forward. This is healthy! You should talk about your differences when you have them and work through them together.

Perhaps one of your friends has found herself in a pickle (that is Southern speak for a tough situation), and you felt uncomfortable standing by her. You knew in your heart the right thing to do was stand with her, but you felt embarrassed at the attention her tough situation put on you. Sometimes when we feel uncomfortable, we ignore the problem or sift to the back of the crowd until the problem dies down. Is that what a good friend does?

Peter did this with Jesus in spite of the fact that Peter loved him very much!

> Now Peter was sitting out in the courtyard, and a servant girl came to him. "You also were with Jesus of Galilee," she said. But he denied it before them all. "I don't know what you're talking about," he said. Then he went out to the gateway, where another servant girl saw him and said to the people there, "This fellow was with Jesus of Nazareth."
>
> He denied it again, with an oath: "I don't know the man!" After a little while, those standing there went up to Peter and said, "Surely you are one of them; your accent gives you away." Then he began to call down curses, and he swore to them, "I don't know the man!" Immediately a rooster crowed. Then Peter remembered the word Jesus had spoken: "Before the rooster crows, you will disown me three times." And he went outside and wept bitterly.
>
> Matt. 26:69–75 (NIV)

Peter felt peer pressure! He was surrounded by people who did not like Jesus, and Peter was afraid of what they might do to him if the crowd knew they were friends. He made a regretful choice. Did Peter recognize his poor decision? Look again! He knew immediately—and wept at the result of his choice to deny his friendship with Jesus.

It is easy for us to say, "Oh, I would never do that!" The truth, though, is we are all guilty of making rotten choices from time to time. We make poor decisions on occasion because we are human and live in a broken world. Sadly, we can all relate to this situation. It is very possible you have been the friend who denied another, but you have likely also been the friend who was neglected. These decisions hurt both people in the friendship.

Did Jesus forgive Peter? He sure did, because true friends are able to say, "I am sorry," and "I forgive you." More importantly, true friends say these words and mean them. When Jesus rose from the dead and faced Peter again, do you think he shook his head and said, "Peter, I still cannot believe you did that to me!"? No! When he forgave Peter, he truly forgave him.

You have probably heard the saying, "That is easier said than done." It is true. When someone hurts us, it is not always easy to forgive the person who did the hurting. Trust is broken. We need God to help us through our feelings of hurt. And while we may forgive, rebuilding trust may take time. This is okay, girls. Healing may take longer than we anticipate, but the important thing is that we do forgive and allow God to heal our hurts.

We also do not forgive only for the sake of forgiving. Rather, we forgive because God calls us to love one another. We cannot love one another if we hold on to anger. It is through God that we are able to move past the hurt and try to see others as he sees them.

> *But the Holy Spirit produces this kind of fruit in our lives: love, joy, peace, patience, kindness, goodness, faithfulness, gentleness, and self-control. There is no law against these things!*
>
> Gal. 5:22–23 NLT

Can you imagine how beautiful our world would be if everyone cultivated the fruit of their spirits? Just like the fruit we eat, the fruit of our spirits must be nurtured. We are able nurture our fruit by practicing each of these qualities.

Close Connections

Remember, we allow our friends to see parts of ourselves that we would not show to just anyone. I am going to repeat a snippet from Chapter Two, because it is super important, girls!

Anytime we share a part of ourselves, we show vulnerability or openness. Anytime you open your heart, there is the risk that you will get hurt. This may have already happened to you. This is why it is so important to choose your friends carefully. Because we want to contribute to our friends' well-being, we tend to care a great deal about how our friends feel and what they think about us. This is okay, but it can be dangerous when the friendship is not healthy.

Have you heard that little voice inside you that helps guide your decision-making? That voice is the Holy Spirit guiding you—the soft whisper inside that you hear saying, "I probably should not do this, but . . ." I cannot tell you how many times my mom and dad asked me to reflect on this verse: "Don't be fooled by those who say such things, for 'bad company corrupts good character'" (1 Cor. 15:33 NLT).

Some friends in your life will encourage you to do things and say things you know in your heart are wrong. You have a choice. You *always* have a choice. No one said that choice would be easy, either. Even though you may think this friend is really fun, she may not be as good a friend if she is asking you to do things that dishonor yourself, your other friends, or most importantly, God.

When you make a choice to listen to the voice inside your spirit that encourages you to select the action that you know in your heart is right, you run the risk that this friend may not want to hang out with you anymore. If making a good choice were easy, our world would be a much different place. With God's help (and the support of your parents and other friends), you can make the choice to forge relationships with people who encourage you to be the person God has designed you to be.

Walk with the wise and become wise; associate with fools and get in trouble.

Prov. 13:20 NLT

Let us say you make a very difficult choice to spend time apart from a friend you know has negatively influenced some of your recent decisions. What happens next? Do you stop caring for her and being nice to her? No! Even if she is not nice to you, remember that you have control over your own behavior and how you respond to her. Again, her choices reflect her character, and how you respond when her choices affect you reflects yours.

Look back at the fruits of the Spirit again. Just because you are not spending time hanging out with someone you once did does not mean you have to stop acknowledging his or her presence. Try to take the opportunity to be a *positive* influence in a way that is healthy for both of you. This may look like saying hi in the hallway or wishing someone a happy birthday at school even though you are not going to that person's birthday festivities. You may loan a pencil to this person before a test, or let him or her go first in line at the water fountain.

Dare to be different. Remember your friend (or former friend) may not respond as you do after that tough choice to stop spending as much time together. However, your kindness in spite of their sour attitude may plant a seed for change that blossoms later down the road. Perhaps God brought you into their life for a short season to plant a seed that he will enable others to cultivate and grow. Your only job with this individual is to lovingly plant a tiny seed. Even if you will not be present for the beautiful blooming that eventually occurs, open your heart to opportunities where God may ask you to serve the kingdom in this way. They can be transformative experiences for you, too.

 girl of grace HeaRT CHeCK

♥ How does it feel when we do not stick by a friend through a tough situation when we know in our hearts we really should?

♥ What impact does this choice have on the friend in need? Perhaps you have been the person let down by her friends. How did you feel when your favored companions did not stand by you? Mom?

♥ Do you have a friend who encourages you to be anything other than the girl of grace God has created you to be? Talk with Mom about why being friends with this person is important to you.

♥ Is the relationship you just described healthy, or is it time to make a tough choice? Pray with Mom and ask God for the wisdom to make the choice that will honor him and the girl of grace he has designed you to be.

♥ Brainstorm with mom on ways you can cultivate the fruits of the Spirit within your own heart. Refer to Galatians 5:22–23.

♥ Read Galatians 5:22–23 again and write it in the space below.

♥ Which quality is your greatest fruit-bearing trait? Take turns with Mom discussing what you think.

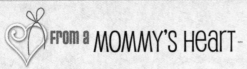
When my oldest munchkin was in preschool, she begged and begged us to let her get her hair cut short. There were three little friends at school who had chin-length hair, and they called themselves the "Short Hair Club." My little girl longed to be part of this group, and she asked for months before we relented.

We picked a long weekend from school for the big event. My husband and I asked if she was sure she wanted to cut her long hair, and she smiled brightly while saying, "Yes!" So off to the beauty salon we went. She could not have been more proud of her new cut, and my husband and I had to admit she looked adorable.

She could not wait for the next preschool day so she could show her friends her new cut. When that next Tuesday finally arrived, she skipped from the car all the way to her classroom. I kissed her and left. When I picked my little one up in the drive-through line, her face was down, and I could tell she was crying. After giving her a big hug and getting her buckled, I asked why she was sad.

With quivering chin, she looked up with tears in her eyes and said, "They wouldn't play with me because my hair isn't yellow." Gulp. I wanted to cry. Actually, I think I did curl up with my husband after my daughter was in bed that night and weep for her broken heart. I held her when we got home from school and talked with her about how sometimes we say and do things that hurt others, and sometimes others do and say things to hurt us. Whether intentional or not, the result is the same.

She recovered and found other friends to play with at school. However, that experience changed something in her. My daughter is sensitive about how words affect others. I do wish the care she has with others translated more often to her baby sis, but overall she is a tender, compassionate person. She recognizes that words have power, and our words can build up or destroy other people.

Friendships and experiences like the one my daughter went through help mold us into the adults we become. We cannot always see how God is at work in our lives through the development of friendships, but that does not mean he is not working. The experience my baby girl went through that day so many years ago left a scar on my mommy heart. Understanding that God is at work in my children's lives is a thought and prayer never far from my mind. However, my mommy heart hurts when one of my babies is in pain.

Gosh, can you imagine how magnified this feeling must be for the God who so lovingly created us? One of my most painful—and I stress _painful_—heartbreaks through friendship happened after I was full-grown and married. We are never immune to the risk of hurt. As an adult, though, I sat and wept in the arms of Jesus instead of the arms of my mom.

We will not always be physically present to hold our kids and tell them everything will be okay, but God will! I say it often, ladies, and I will say it again. I am a girl of grace in training just like the rest of you. Perhaps what we need to remember in moments of hurt like this is that God created us for community. He understands our need for companionship. Who better to fulfill that need than the One who made us what and who we are? My prayer is that my girls will continue to love and nurture a relationship with Christ and that he will be the friend they seek in all seasons of life.

say
WHAT?

In the beginning, God created the heavens and the earth.
The earth was without form and void, and darkness
was over the face of the deep. And the Spirit of God was
hovering over the face of the waters.
And God said, "Let there be light," and there was light.

Gen. 1:1–3 ESV

WOrds have power, friends. We know this because our God literally spoke our world into being. As God's image bearers, our words have power, too. Of all the creatures on this planet, only people have the ability to communicate through the spoken word. The power to use words is a unique and potent gift from God.

Remember Peter Parker's uncle said, "With great power comes great responsibility." Boy, is that the truth! Jesus tells us in the book of Matthew that on the Day of Judgment, we will be held accountable for the words we have spoken (Matt. 12:36–37). Words are so important that we will be asked to give an account of what we have said when we stand before the Lord.

Mom can probably share with you words she remembers that were spoken to her from when she was your age—whether positive or negative. Spoken words have the power to affirm and destroy. When we are rebuking the enemy, we do not only think the words in our head, "In Jesus's name, get thee behind me, Satan!" No! We say the words aloud, because they have power.

As Christians, we are called to let the power of our words manifest the power of our faith (1 Pet. 3:15). When we accept Jesus into our hearts, we allow ourselves to be transformed by God and his truth. This includes our actions, our thoughts, *and* our choice of words.

Think about this in the context of your circles of grace. We use words as one of our primary modes of communication. It would be tough to build and sustain relationships on our actions and body language alone. If you were to try to make it through one day without speaking one word (including our signing friends—those are still words), it would be really tough. We need *words* to help us share and connect.

Is it easy to discern whether our words are affirming or not? Sometimes, seemingly innocent words have the potential to hurt someone else, even if they were not ill-intentioned. This happens when our words shift from sharing to gossip.

What is the Difference between Gossip and Sharing?

We have talked about how God created us out of love, and we know he created us for community. We are designed to be social creatures. No, that does not mean every one of us will love a good party. It means that on some level, we each desire to be connected to other people in some way. Being connected means we like to share part of ourselves. In other words, we like spending time together and talking with the people in our circle.

So what kinds of things do we talk about with our friends? I do not know about you, but I like to talk with my friends about a little bit of everything. When I am with my favorite gal pals, we chat about anything and everything. Sometimes, we talk about what is happening in our day-to-day lives, but other times we may talk about what is happening with other friends or people we know. It could be something like, "Did you hear Mary Jane is going out of town next week? Her grandmother is really sick." Being friends or being part of a community tends to mean you like to know what is going on with the people in your circle of grace.

There is nothing wrong with being interested in other people's lives. God designed us to crave these types of connections, because he longs to be connected to each one of us on a daily basis, too. God gets it! But how do you know when sharing becomes gossiping? According to Google, gossip is "casual or unconstrained conversation or reports about other people, typically involving details that are not confirmed as being true."

We have all been there. Whether we were the one talking about someone else or simply listening to the juicy tidbit that someone else was sharing behind another person's back, gossiping is a dangerous pastime. Have you ever been part of a conversation that started something like this, "Did you hear what Beth said about Susan?" Look back at the definition of gossip. It is not a simple sharing of information or concern for another person. Gossip is "casual or unrestrained conversation or reports about other people, typically involving details that are not confirmed as being true." Let us dig deeper, girls.

The Bible has much to say on the topic of gossip. Look first at Exodus 23:1–2.

> *You must not spread a false report. Do not join the*
> *wicked to be a malicious witness. You must not follow a*
> *crowd in wrongdoing. Do not testify in a lawsuit and go*
> *along with a crowd to pervert justice.*
>
> Exod. 23:1–2 HCSB

What does this passage mean? Think about a group of people sitting around the lunch table. Someone at the table begins to talk about another classmate, and you know what this person is saying is not true. But then again, this is your circle of friends. You do not want to rock the boat by being the person to say they are spreading a rumor that is untrue, so you stay silent. What you have done is help spread a false report! You went along with the crowd, even though you knew in your heart it was wrong, because you wanted to avoid conflict.

It has happened to all of us. You know why? We are not perfect. Every one of us has been in a situation we wished we had handled differently when it was all said and done—but that is why we need that little voice inside of us that helps guide our choices. Remember, that little voice is the Holy Spirit. Gossiping can be hurtful. Perhaps you have been on the receiving end of the scenario we just discussed.

Have you heard the saying, "Sticks and stones may break my bones, but words will never hurt me"? It is *so* not true. Our words have immense power. We already know that God literally spoke our world into being (Gen. 1:1–3). Proverbs 16:27 reminds us that gossip can be damaging because words have the power to wound our spirit: "Mean people spread mean gossip; their words smart and burn" (*The Message*). We discussed in Chapter One how we must care for our spiritual selves just as we care for our physical selves. Words may not damage our physical bodies, but they have the power to decimate our spirits.

Sometimes we do not even realize the lasting impact our words have on other people. Affirming words can be just as powerful as hurtful gossip, so given a choice—which will you choose to share with others?

girl of grace HEarT CHECK

♥ Write Hebrews 11:3 in the space below. What does this passage say about the power of the spoken word?

♥ Talk with Mom about the difference between sharing and gossiping.

♥ How can gossip harm your circle of grace?

♥ Is it possible to speak against gossip with confidence? Brainstorm with Mom about ways you can do this with your own circle of friends.

♥ Can you think of a time when you participated in gossip about another friend or person? How did your actions impact the object of your discussions? How did you feel? Mom, what about you?

♥ Look up Matthew 12:34–37. Do you agree our hearts determine what we say? Do you think this is a good thing or a dangerous thing? Talk with Mom about why or why not.

♥ How can you use your words to make a positive impact in your circle of grace? What about beyond your circle? Be sure Mom gets a turn to share, too!

an activity for mom and me: POSITIVE AFFIRMATION

Read James 3:1–12, and pay close attention to what the Bible says here about the power of the tongue.

> Dear brothers and sisters, not many of you should become teachers in the church, for we who teach will be judged more strictly. Indeed, we all make many mistakes. For if we could control our tongues, we would be perfect and could also control ourselves in every other way.
>
> We can make a large horse go wherever we want by means of a small bit in its mouth. And a small rudder makes a huge ship turn wherever the pilot chooses to go, even though the winds are strong. In the same way, the tongue is a small thing that makes grand speeches.
>
> But a tiny spark can set a great forest on fire. And among all the parts of the body, the tongue is a flame of fire. It is a whole world of wickedness, corrupting your entire body. It can set your whole life on fire, for it is set on fire by hell itself.

i can't Believe you Said That!

When someone hurts you, sometimes you want to hurt him or her in return by firing back ugly words. You may think it will make you feel better, but oftentimes engaging in a battle of angry words only makes the situation worse. (Think back to James's observation that "a tiny spark can set a great forest on fire.") Has this ever happened to you? It stings to hear that someone you thought was a friend has been talking behind your back. What do you do when this happens? Do you go to another mutual friend and lament to that person about the friend who was talking about you?

It may sound strange, but the act of gossip has been around a long, long time. Our methods of communication may have evolved over time, but human

People can tame all kinds of animals, birds, rep-tiles, and fish, but no one can tame the tongue. It is restless and evil, full of deadly poison. Sometimes it praises our Lord and Father, and sometimes it curses those who have been made in the image of God.
And so blessing and cursing come pouring out of the same mouth. Surely, my brothers and sisters, this is not right! Does a spring of water bubble out with both fresh water and bitter water? Does a fig tree produce olives, or a grapevine produce figs? No, and you can't draw fresh water from a salty spring.

James 3:1–12 NLT

Talk with Mom about what this passage means to each of you. Specifically, what does it mean by "a tiny spark can set a great forest on fire"?

We have a choice as to what kind of impact our words have on others. This week's Mom and Me activity is about consciously using our tongues for positive affirmation of other people. There are so many fun ways this activity can take form! Be creative and do not limit your acts of positive affirmation to one person. You might be surprised by how much fun you have lifting up other people in and outside of your circle of grace!

nature remains unchanged. The fact that the Bible has much to share on the topic is evidence to us that this is not a new social dilemma. When someone hurts you, sometimes you want to hurt him or her in return by firing back ugly words. You may think it will make you feel better, but oftentimes engaging in a battle of angry words only makes the situation worse. (Think back to James's observation that "a tiny spark can set a great forest on fire.")

Don't testify against your neighbors without cause; don't lie about them. And don't say, "Now I can pay them back for what they've done to me! I'll get even with them!"

Prov. 24:28–29 NLT)

This is one of those tough situations in life that really does not get easier to work through as we grow older. This is why we need Jesus, girls. Even adults struggle to make a good choice about how to use their words positively with others when they feel hurt or betrayed. We say things in anger on occasion that we may not have dared to utter if we were calm. God understands our hearts, and how blessed are we to have a loving God who never runs out of patience with us!

Friends disagree, and it is okay to take a breath and distance yourself in order to pray and think through the best way to respond when someone has said something to hurt or anger you. Jesus often sought a quiet place to pray and reflect.

We all make mistakes, and chances are pretty good that you and a friend have disagreed over something one of you said at one time or another. When this happens, the best policy is always to talk your differences through with the person who has hurt or angered you. If you are the one who has done the hurting—whether intentionally or not—try to work through your argument face-to-face.

We may be tempted to share our grievances with other friends who lend a sympathetic ear, but this can be a dangerous practice. Venting to friends who were not involved in your argument can easily be construed as gossip, even if that is honestly not your intention. What if word of your venting session made it back to the friend you were angry with? When you lament to that uninvolved friend, he or she might wonder if you are venting about *them* to someone else. Or what if you were on the other end and heard that your friend was talking about your disagreement with other people? How would that make you feel?

If you need a safe place to talk, consider confiding in your mom or another safe adult who is highly unlikely to share your story with anyone else. God placed these people in your life for a reason—they are there to share your concerns, to pray with you and for you. They are also likely able and willing to lend guidance in a situation where you feel overwhelmed and support you through the reconciliation and healing process.

Troublemakers start fights; gossips break up friendships.
Prov. 16:28 *The Message*)

Gossiping can really hurt your circle of grace. Misunderstandings happen—of course! However, if you have a friend who constantly likes to talk about other people for the sake of talking about them, it is time to take a stand. Again, these are not always easy choices to make, but remember you are not standing alone. God is with you, but so are your parents and other members of your circle of grace.

When I was in the fourth grade, a group of girls that lived near me loved to ride bikes around our area of town. It seems like we spent every spare minute riding our bikes and making up fun games to play. Well, a new girl moved to town about that time. She was probably excited to learn that there were several other girls her age nearby. We were not tough to spot, especially since we rode past her house practically every day.

Some of my friends did not like the new girl, though, and I honestly cannot remember why. They were just adamant that she should not ride bikes with us. Well, one of my friends decided to let the new girl know she was not welcome by leaving a note one day in the basket of her bike that she left parked outside her house. I cannot remember what the note said, as I did not write it. I was there, though, when the note was delivered. I was there when we rode away from the new girl's house to embark on our daily bicycle adventure.

I arrived home that day to a very angry father who had gotten a phone call from the new girl's mother. She had called all our parents to read the note and let them know what my group of friends had done. I made a poor choice by participating in an activity that intentionally hurt someone else, but I was angry that the new girl's mom called our parents. Most of us lost privileges to ride our bikes, and we were told to apologize to our new neighbor in person.

My dad said something to me that day that has always stuck with me. He asked me if I had heard of the Golden Rule—to which I replied, "No." We looked up Matthew 7:12 together. Here is what it says:

> *Here is a simple, rule-of-thumb guide for behavior: Ask yourself what you want people to do for you, then grab the initiative and do it for* them. *Add up God's Law and Prophets and this is what you get.*
>
> *The Message*

My dad shed a light on an important life lesson for me, and I can honestly say this is something I still strive daily to live by. My dad flipped the situation around on me, and he made me think about how I would have felt as the new girl. It was not a pleasant self-reflection, but I am so glad now that the new girl's mom called my parents. It changed my perspective, and the new girl and I actually became really good friends.

However, not all my other friends who rode bikes so often with me felt the same way. They returned to school and made sure to share with as many people as they could how awful this new person was and why no one should like her or be nice to her. It definitely was not an easy and painless process, but with God's help and my parents' support, I stopped hanging out with a lot of the girls I had spent so much time with in the past. I did not like the choices they were making, and more importantly, I did not like the "me" I was when we hung out together. I started spending time with the new girl and other friends.

Five years later, I was the new girl—in a new city in a new state at a new school. The new girl from fourth grade had become one of my very best friends, and we wrote constantly to keep each other informed of the latest and greatest in one another's lives. That kind of friendship stands the test of time and distance, and those are connections for which we should be extremely thankful. They are rare and special.

 girl of grace Heart check

♥ Read Ecclesiastes 7:21–22 and write it in the space below.

♥ Can you and Mom take turns sharing a time when something like this happened to you?

♥ Have you ever said something about someone that you did not have the courage to say directly to that person? How did you handle it?

♥ Would you do things differently now? Share with Mom how you can handle this differently should it happen again.

♥ Do you have a friend who likes to talk about other people when they're not there?

♥ Talk with Mom about ways you can positively affirm this friend and stand up against gossiping. Is this something you think you can do? Why or why not?

From a MOMMY'S HEART

Oh, mamas. This is a <u>tough</u> topic! If only we could keep our baby girls from feeling the sting of gossip and hurtful words. When my oldest darling was in kindergarten, she was one of the quieter kiddos in class. Being quiet allowed her to observe all kinds of details about others, and she determined pretty quickly whom she wanted to play with during recess.

One of the girls in her class did not care for my daughter. Every day, my little girl would climb into my car and share what difficult experience had transpired during class that day. One day, she climbed into my car in tears. It broke my heart.

Now, I have to interrupt my story for a moment to tell you that my husband and I are die-hard Aggies. As you may know, college football is a <u>big</u> deal in the South. I grew up in Louisiana, but something went awry in my genetic makeup—as I do not bleed LSU (Louisiana State University) purple and gold. I bleed Texas A&M's maroon and white! My parents will tell you I always wanted to attend Texas A&M, so it was a huge blessing when my family relocated to Texas in high school. That dream became a reality. My husband and I have done our best to share our love of Aggieland with our girls. I even played the Aggie War Hymn in the car on the way to work every day when I was pregnant with my oldest daughter (remember, no judgment—only love). Ironically, it was one of the only things that kept her calm in the car after she arrived. But I digress. My oldest darling was not (and is not) shy about supporting the Texas Aggies. Now, back to my story . . .

My daughter said this little girl from her class had called her an ugly name all day at school. She even told other friends that my daughter was this bad word, and they all started calling her this name. Well, I admit I was all too curious as to what awful word had circulated in the kindergarten classroom that day. I asked my daughter if she could tell me what the word was, and she shook her head vigorously, saying, "No! It's too bad to say out loud." I thought for a moment. She sniffled from the backseat and softly said, "I think I could draw it for you, Mommy." Now I was really stumped.

I fished a piece of paper and a pen out of my purse and handed them back to my little girl. After a few minutes, she passed the paper back to me. I remember staring at the paper and turning it to see if I could make out the word she had drawn as a picture for me.

"Is it a ghost?" I asked. "No," she replied. I stared for a moment longer.

Then it dawned on me. "Is it a longhorn?" I asked. My sweet baby girl burst into tears and cried, "Yes! Isn't it awful?" (For those who do not follow college football, Texas A&M's primary rival for years and years was the Texas Longhorns.)

I tried to hide my smile while replying, "Aw, honey. That would have hurt my feelings, too."

My husband and I still chuckle at this story, but this was really my oldest daughter's first encounter with gossip. Words have power, and ugly words can leave a permanent scar on our hearts. As funny as this story was, we used the experience to help our daughter learn the importance of imparting words of affirmation. We are all guilty of making poor choices, and trust me, I make them with alarming frequency. We also have the ability to make really positive ones. Choosing to use words to affirm instead of using them to wound is a life lesson that we cannot stress enough with our tween darlings.

My prayer is that one of the many conversations my husband and I share with our girls will imprint on their hearts just like the conversation my daddy had with me all those years ago. As parents, we have the ability to speak positive, powerful words into our children's spirits. Let us not miss an opportunity to build up these amazing creatures who have been entrusted into our care.

CHapTer 5

i Will
IF YOU WILL!

"My child, if sinners entice you,
turn your back on them!
My child, don't go along with them!
Stay far away from their paths."

Prov. 1:10, 15 NLT

OUr CirCleS OF grACe are a beautiful reflection of the people we love and who love us. We know our circles consist of both relationships we choose for ourselves and relationships that are selected for us (by God, our parents, our church, and so on). We care what the people within our circles think, and we invest a great deal of ourselves into building strong relationships with them. Why? God created us for community, and we desire to be connected to other people in some way.

Our circles reflect *community*. The really cool thing about this is that community is one of the most important ways we embody Jesus Christ on earth. When we love and accept one another, we shine Christ's light. When we inevitably hurt one another, then ask and accept forgiveness, we reflect Christ's grace. In his perfect love, Christ has already forgiven us.

Briefly, let's recall who is at the center of your circle. It is you! At the heart of you is God. He already knows your heart, because he lovingly crafted it and knit every fiber of you in your mother's tummy. Even though God created you and knows your heart, he still wants *you* to know *him*. He longs to spend time with you, holding on to your deepest secrets and sharing your greatest dreams. How do we connect with God? We connect with God in much the same way we connect with others.

So how do we connect with our friends or other people we want to know better? We discover ways in which we are similar, right? You and your gal pals may share many of the same likes and dislikes when it comes to music, clothes, school subjects, and more. The more you have in common, the more time you may spend together—for that very reason. Your interests draw you together. As God's image bearer, think of how much you have in common with him.

Understanding Who influences me

Your friends or peers influence your life—even if you do not realize it—just by spending time with you. It is perfectly normal to listen to your friends and find interest in their lives. You learn from one another. People from your peer group may not even be your friends (those favored companions), but perhaps you hold them in high regard—such as other students from your school or even a celebrity your age.

Peers can have a positive influence on each other. Maybe you are super excited about a new book you are reading, and after you tell your friends all about it, they are excited and have started reading it as well. Or perhaps there is someone at school or church who is always doing something nice for other people, and others try to be more like him or her. Maybe there is a friend or someone you know who is incredibly talented at a sport you like, and you are inspired to be more like them. It is possible another student who is a whiz at math has taught an easy way to remember a tricky math formula to someone else who is struggling. All these examples are positive ways that peers influence one another every single day.

However, peers also have the ability to influence each other in negative ways. For example, a group of your friends may not like another student and encourage you to not be nice to that person or exclude him or her from sitting with your circle during lunch or recess. Or perhaps a peer asked you for help to cheat on an exam because he or she forgot to study. It could happen at a sleepover with girlfriends when the girl talk steers to gossip and mean-spirited conversations about other people who are not present. Or even worse, the group could exclude a person who is present and allow her to overhear their ugly words with the sole purpose of wounding her.

When peers try to influence how you act—whether intentionally or not—it is called peer pressure. Think back to the story of when Peter denied Jesus! This is something we all encounter, and it does not necessarily get easier as we grow older. Your mom can likely share plenty of examples with you of how she continues to encounter instances of peer pressure as an adult. Not only have we all experienced peer pressure as the person being influenced, but we have also been the person trying to influence the decision of someone else.

Have you ever uttered these words? "Oh, come on! I really want you to do this with me!" I bet you have! Remember, peer pressure can be positive or negative. Take a peek at another example the Bible shares with us. A woman named Lydia demonstrates an awesome example of positive peer pressure in her story from Acts 16.

> We [Paul and his companions] boarded a boat at Troas and sailed straight across to the island of Samothrace, and the next day we landed at Neapolis. From there we reached Philippi, a major city of that district of Macedonia and a Roman colony. And we stayed there several days.
>
> On the Sabbath we went a little way outside the city to a riverbank, where we thought people would be meeting for prayer, and we sat down to speak with some women who had gathered there. One of them was Lydia from Thyatira, a merchant of expensive purple cloth, who worshiped God. As she listened to us, the Lord opened her heart, and she accepted what Paul was saying. She and her household were baptized, and she asked us to be her guests. "If you agree that I am a true believer in the Lord," she said, "come and stay at my home." And she urged us until we agreed.
>
> Acts 16:11–15 NLT

Lydia was a merchant of expensive purple cloth, which meant she was probably very wealthy. She likely had a large household who followed her direction without question. This passage from the Bible happened in the early days of the Christian church when professing your faith was dangerous. Although there were several women present, Lydia is the only woman mentioned by name. We learn that Lydia's entire household was baptized after she opened her heart to the Lord. And look at the last line of this passage. Lydia asked Paul and Silas to be her guests, and it goes so far as to say, "She urged us until we agreed." What Lydia used was peer pressure!

Our friend Lydia is mentioned again toward the end of this chapter.

> But Paul replied, "They have publicly beaten us without a trial and put us in prison—and we are Roman citizens. So now they want us to leave secretly? Certainly not! Let them come themselves to release us!"

When the police reported this, the city officials were alarmed to learn that Paul and Silas were Roman citizens. So they came to the jail and apologized to them. Then they brought them out and begged them to leave the city. When Paul and Silas left the prison, they returned to the home of Lydia. There they met with the believers and encouraged them once more. Then they left town.

Acts 16:37–40 NLT

As you read through Acts 16, it becomes clear through Paul and Silas's journey just how dangerous it was to spread the gospel in the early days of the Christian church. Yet, in spite of the dangers, Lydia opened her home to other believers as a meeting place. Talk about a positive influence! Lydia was likely a very wealthy community member who had many slaves and a large household. Think of the positive peer influence she had on others, as she stood strong in her faith despite the danger of doing so publicly.

Lydia sets a great example for us. We do not know for sure, but the passages that mention her suggest Lydia's faith was more important to her than what others thought. Is not that what matters most? We were created by a loving God who wants nothing more than to have a relationship with each of us. The Bible reinforces this truth in numerous passages, including this one from Galatians. "Am I now trying to win the approval of human beings, or of God? Or am I trying to please people? If I were still trying to please people, I would not be a servant of Christ" (Gal. 1:10 NIV).

 girl of grace HEART CHECK

♥ As God's image bearer, make a list of things you have in common with our Creator. Mom, you, too.

💜 Share your experience of peer pressure with Mom. Can you relate to any of the examples shared earlier in this chapter? If yes, explain how so.

💜 When was a time you felt negative peer pressure among your circle? How did you handle it?

💜 What are some positive ways you can influence the actions of others? Mom, you share, too!

💜 Talk with Mom about how to be a positive peer influencer even when others around you seem unreceptive.

You have brainstormed ways to positively influence the action of your peers in the Girl of Grace Heart Check. Now it is time to put those ideas into action!

This week's Mom and Me activity is about taking the lead within your peer group and influencing others to make a positive choice or action. Here are a few ideas to help get you started if you had a tough time brainstorming on your own.

- ♥ Organize a group of your peers (and their moms) to volunteer at a local serving center.
- ♥ Join a sport you have wanted to try and encourage a peer to go with you.
- ♥ Set aside your phone and pick up a book instead, but do this when others around you seem engaged in their phones.
- ♥ Influence connectivity in person instead of online.
- ♥ Instead of gossiping, encourage your friends to talk about others in a positive way.
- ♥ Offer to help around the house without being asked and encourage a sibling to help you.

Setting a positive example for others is rewarding for you as well. Have fun and talk with Mom about how consciously working to influence the action of others in a positive way makes you feel.

Facing negative peer pressure

Unfortunately, peer pressure can also have a negative influence on our choices. How do you take a stand when you feel pressured to act in a way that you know is wrong?

Do you remember the story of Noah? Chances are you have heard the Bible story of Noah and the ark. God's heart was sad at what the world had become during the time Noah lived, and he sent a great flood to wipe out all that he had created and begin again. Before God sent the flood, he asked a faithful man named Noah to build a great boat that could hold his entire family, along with two of every kind of living thing on earth. Can you imagine how big this boat must have been? The Bible tells us how large it was (Gen. 6:15), and scholars believe it took decades for Noah to build.

Noah lived in a part of the world that did not see much rain, and it is likely that Noah's neighbors did not understand at all why he was building such a large boat. The Bible does not tell us specifically that Noah was ridiculed, but put yourself inside the story. If you lived in a desert climate where there was little to no rain, would you think it was silly to see someone building a huge boat in preparation for a great flood? Not only that, but imagine this person was also collecting two of every kind of living creature to put inside the boat when there was absolutely no sign of rain. You might think he was crazy!

Friends and neighbors probably teased Noah mercilessly as he spent literally years and years building a boat as God asked him to do. Did Noah give in to the peer pressure of others and give up building the ark? No! We know from the Bible that Noah did, in fact, finish the ark. He honored the request God made of him, and he gathered all the creatures and loaded them onto the boat. What happened when the boat was built and the animals and Noah's family were loaded safely on board? God sent the rain.

Noah models for us how to stand against peer pressure and follow the path God has asked. It could not have been easy for Noah, but he lived for God—not for the favor of mankind. God rewarded Noah for his faithfulness.

The Bible is full of other examples, but look closer at Pontius Pilate, the Roman leader who sentenced Jesus to death. Like Noah, Pontius Pilate struggled against peer pressure. However, unlike Noah, Pontius Pilate ultimately succumbed to the influence of others—making a decision he would later regret. His story is found in the book of Matthew.

> *Then Jesus stood in front of the leader of the country. The leader asked Jesus, "Are You the King of the Jews?" Jesus said to him, "What you say is true." When the head religious leaders and the other leaders spoke against Him, He said nothing. Then Pilate said to Him, "Do You not hear all these things they are saying against You?" Jesus did not say a word. The leader was much surprised and wondered about it.*
>
> *At the special supper each year the leader of the country would always let one person who was in prison go*

free. It would be the one the people wanted. They had a man who was known by all the people whose name was Barabbas. When they were gathered together, Pilate said to them, "Whom do you want me to let go free? Should it be Barabbas or Jesus Who is called Christ?" For the leader of the country knew the religious leaders had given Jesus over to him because they were jealous.

While Pilate was sitting in the place where he judges, his wife sent him this word, "Have nothing to do with that good Man. I have been troubled today in a dream about Him."

The head religious leaders and the other leaders talked the many people into asking for Barabbas to go free and for Jesus to be put to death. The leader of the country said to them, "Which one of the two do you want me to let go free?" They said, "Barabbas." Pilate said to them, "Then what am I to do with Jesus Who is called Christ?" They all said to him, "Nail Him to a cross!" Then Pilate said, "Why, what bad thing has He done?" But they cried out all the more, "Nail Him to a cross!"

Pilate saw that he could do nothing. The people were making loud calls and there was much pushing around. He took water and washed his hands in front of the many people. He said, "I am not guilty of the blood of this good Man. This is your own doing." Then all the people said, "Let His blood be on us and on our children!" Pilate let Barabbas go free but he had men whip Jesus. Then he handed Him over to be nailed to a cross.

Matt. 27:11–26 NLV

Barabbas was a well-known murderer, and Pontius Pilate knew this. Through his story in the Bible, we learn that Pontius Pilate wanted to set Jesus free. The angry crowd gathered outside his office felt otherwise, though, and they made their intentions blatantly clear. So although Pontius Pilate disagreed with the choice, he gave in to the will of the crowd and sent Jesus to his death.

Pontius Pilate is an extreme example of giving in to negative peer pressure. Thankfully, we do not encounter life or death situations on a daily basis as the people we read about in the Bible did. Professing faith was—and sometimes still can be—an unpopular choice, but that does not make standing up for your faith the wrong choice. God equips us with everything we need to stand strong against others who would encourage us to make objectionable choices.

When you feel pressured to make a choice that goes along with the crowd, but you know in your heart it is the wrong decision, take a moment to pray and ask God for strength to make the right choice. The choice that honors God and reflects positively on the girl of grace he has called you to be. Yes, it is true. Making the unpopular or unusual choice could result in negative repercussions from the group who encouraged you to choose an alternative option. However, you are very possibly lending positive influence to someone else who is looking for the courage to stand up in that very same way.

Remember our example in the last chapter about sitting around the lunch table when one of your friends begins to talk about another person in an unflattering way? Instead of remaining mum, you could model positive peer pressure by using your words to stop the negative talk. Your positive influence may help give courage to someone else at the table who also wanted to take a stand.

> *You must not follow the crowd in doing wrong. When you*
> *are called to testify in a dispute, do not be swayed by the*
> *crowd to twist justice. And do not slant your testimony in*
> *favor of a person just because that person is poor.*
>
> Exod. 23:2–3 NLT)

 girl of grace HearT CHeCK

♥ Read 1 Corinthians 15:33. Talk with Mom about what this passage means to you and write your thoughts below.

♥ Talk with Mom about the difference between positive and negative peer pressure.

♥ What are examples of negative peer pressure you have experienced? How did you handle it? Could you have done anything differently?

♥ Mom, what about you? Do you think getting older means you will not encounter peer pressure? Talk with your daughter about why or why not.

♥ What are the dangers of peer pressure and allowing others to influence our decision-making?

♥ Make a list of how you can positively influence the actions of people who encourage you to make questionable choices.

▶

▶

▶

▶

▶

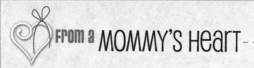

We are all familiar with crowd mentality. The phrase can be misleading, as it sometimes conjures images like the one of the angry mob demanding Barabbas's release from Pontius Pilate. However, crowd mentality can aptly be used to describe connections within our circles of grace.

To me, this is one of the most dangerous forms peer pressure can take. I talked about leaving out the new girl in Chapter Four and that awful day when she discovered the mean note my group of friends left in her bicycle basket. It was not my idea to write or deliver the bad note, but I can remember very distinctly one of my friends rolling her eyes when another of us questioned if going through with this decision was a sound idea. Almost all the girls (and there were seven of us) chimed in that it was not a big deal and to get over ourselves. What happened? An ugly note was delivered to a sweet girl who had no idea what she had done to provoke such mean behavior.

As kids, this type of peer pressure seems harmless, but it is not! Honestly, my husband and I worried often about my oldest darling and her susceptibility to peer pressure due to her quiet nature and very tender spirit. We have often laughed that our youngest darling, who rarely meets a stranger and has no problem telling you what she thinks, would be much better equipped to stand against the influence of others. As they have continued to grow and develop, my husband and I realized we could not be more wrong.

They are both susceptible to peer pressure—just like the rest of us—but in different ways. We are all very different people, so the actions that motivate our decision-making are understandably vast and varied. We are learning our youngest sweet girl actually has a tougher time standing up to the influence of her friends because she cares so much about what they think. Their friendship means so much to her that she would sometimes rather knowingly make a poor choice to keep her friends from being angry with her. As her mama, this terrifies me!

I have had countless conversations with my girls about why it is okay to make an unpopular choice if we know in our hearts the decision we are making is honorable to God, ourselves, and others. When they disagree with friends, it feels huge for them because it is! I do not know anyone who says, "Boy, I hope I get into a fight with my friend today." This is tough stuff, and conflict is painful.

I pray that God gives my husband and me the wisdom to talk with our girls and guide them in their decision-making. No matter how inconsequential the choice may be, we ask, "Have you prayed about it?" Is that not what we do with our friends? We talk with them about all kinds of things and ask for guidance or their thoughts on what we should do about this, that, and the other. My husband and I try to model and talk with our girls about how much God wants us to come to him in the same way.

You have heard me say it plenty, but I do not mind repeating myself. It is good practice for when I am my mom's age (love you, Mama). We are not perfect, and what a good thing to show our kids! The monkey see, monkey do scenario once scared the living daylights out of me—as I know my sweet girls were absorbing everything I did and said. It does not scare me so much anymore. I truly believe God does not waste any experience— good or bad. When I make a mistake, as I so often do, it is an opportunity for me to be real and transparent with my kids.

My daughters do not need a perfect mom. The truth is I am one hot mess-mama, and I am honest with my girls on the days when I have it less than together, which is often. They see me pray for strength. They see me pray for grace. Often, I invite them to pray with me, and they do. How awesome is that?

CHapter 6

no one
LIKeS a BULLY!

Watch the way you talk.
Let nothing foul or dirty come out of your mouth.
Say only what helps, each word a gift.

Eph. 4:29 *The Message*

mean girls and bullies reinforce what we already know. Words can breathe life to affirmation or take the form of barbs that leave scars upon our hearts. Even though tween girls may think their moms are disconnected with what is hip and cool, some things stand the test of time. Mean girls and bullies are not a new phenomenon. Sadly, the truth is many of us will at some point or another be on the receiving end of a mean girl's or bully's hateful taunts.

An encounter with a bully is vastly different than a disagreement with a friend. Stopbullying.gov defines bullying as "unwanted, aggressive behavior among school aged children that involves a real or perceived power imbalance. The behavior is repeated, or has the potential to be repeated, over time." The difference between an argument with a friend and the assault from a bully is in the intention behind the conflict and the repetition of incidents. Bullies exhibit behaviors such as making threats, spreading rumors, attacking someone physically or verbally, and excluding someone from a group on purpose.

The Bible is chock-full of examples of these individuals. We will take a closer look at some of the illustrations we find in the Bible as we dig deeper into this chapter. Before we go any further, though, it is important to shed light on the person who provides the very best example for us about how to respond when we encounter a bully. That person is Jesus. His ministry was epitomized by his courageous willingness to place himself among people in society who were most likely to be taunted—those who were weak and vulnerable, those who were unclean. Many who comprised Jesus's first-century audience would shrink away, as we probably would, at the thought of touching the ugly blind man or dining with the despised community member, like the tax collector

Zacchaeus. Jesus himself was the target of bullies in his day. After his arrest, Jesus was beaten, ridiculed, and even spit upon. Yet, how did he respond?

He responded with kindness and love. He forgave them. He prayed for them. Because of our human brokenness, we cannot respond perfectly like Jesus. However, we *can* try to be more like him. After all, we are his image bearers. Jesus challenges us to rise above our feelings of hurt and hate to love those who persecute us.

> *You're familiar with the old written law, "Love your friend," and its unwritten companion, "Hate your enemy." I'm challenging that. I'm telling you to love your enemies. Let them bring out the best in you, not the worst. When someone gives you a hard time, respond with the energies of prayer, for then you are working out of your true selves, your God-created selves. This is what God does. He gives his best—the sun to warm and the rain to nourish—to everyone, regardless: the good and bad, the nice and nasty. If all you do is love the lovable, do you expect a bonus? Anybody can do that. If you simply say hello to those who greet you, do you expect a medal? Any run-of-the-mill sinner does that. In a word, what I'm saying is, Grow up. You're kingdom subjects. Now live like it. Live out your God-created identity. Live generously and graciously toward others, the way God lives toward you.*

Matt. 5:43–48 *The Message*

Throughout history, two things remain unchanged: God's Word and human nature. God's Word speaks loudly and clearly on the subject of bullying, and the stories we find in the Bible are just as relevant today as the day they were written so long ago. Let's dig deeper.

Why Are They So Mean?

Oh, friends. Haven't we all been there? At some point in each of our lives, chances are highly likely that every single one of us will have an encounter with a bully or mean girl. Even more surprising is sometimes the bully you encounter will be yourself. Shocking, I know! In this chapter, we are going to take a closer look at what type of behavior constitutes a bully or a mean girl in our eyes. What motivates a bully's behavior? We have already talked about the importance of standing up for our friends, but bullies can be tough.

I often heard growing up that bullies were one of those unpleasant but unavoidable experiences that everyone must encounter in life. To some extent, that is true. We cannot control the actions of others and how others choose to behave. However, we do have the freedom to make our own choices, and the Bible provides us with some really great examples of how to cope with situations that involve a person displaying bullying behavior.

What comes to mind when you think of bullies from the Bible? The first example that comes to mind for me is the story of David and Goliath. Take a few minutes to read 1 Samuel 17. Do you think Goliath was a bully?

> *Then Goliath, a Philistine champion from Gath, came out of the Philistine ranks to face the forces of Israel. He was over nine feet tall! He wore a bronze helmet, and his bronze coat of mail weighed 125 pounds. He also wore bronze leg armor, and he carried a bronze javelin on his shoulder. The shaft of his spear was as heavy and thick as a weaver's beam, tipped with an iron spearhead that weighed 15 pounds. His armor bearer walked ahead of him carrying a shield.*
>
> *Goliath stood and shouted a taunt across to the Israelites. "Why are you all coming out to fight?" he called. "I am the Philistine champion, but you are only the servants of Saul. Choose one man to come down here and fight me! If he kills me, then we will be your slaves. But if I kill him, you will be our slaves! I defy the armies of Israel today! Send me a man who will fight me!" When Saul and the Israelites heard this, they were terrified and deeply shaken.*
>
> 1 Sam. 17:4–11 NLT

So what do you think? Was Goliath a bully? Yes! He was definitely a bully. He was physically large, loud, and mean. The Bible tells us that Goliath taunted the Israelites and threatened them. They were afraid of this big giant! He challenged anyone who thought they could beat him in battle to do so, or else the Israelites would be forced into slavery. Even King Saul was worried about how to handle the situation. Isn't that what it feels like when we are faced with standing up to a bully? It can be scary business!

David was the son of a shepherd, and he was just a boy. Yet he had the faith and courage to face Goliath. When David initially approached King Saul, the king quickly denied David's request to stand up to Goliath on behalf of the Israelites. Look what happens:

> "Don't worry about this Philistine," David told Saul. "I'll go fight him!"
>
> "Don't be ridiculous!" Saul replied. "There's no way you can fight this Philistine and possibly win! You're only a boy, and he's been a man of war since his youth."
>
> But David persisted. "I have been taking care of my father's sheep and goats," he said. "When a lion or a bear comes to steal a lamb from the flock, I go after it with a club and rescue the lamb from its mouth. If the animal turns on me, I catch it by the jaw and club it to death. I have done this to both lions and bears, and I'll do it to this pagan Philistine, too, for he has defied the armies of the living God! The LORD who rescued me from the claws of the lion and the bear will rescue me from this Philistine!"
>
> Saul finally consented. "All right, go ahead," he said. "And may the LORD be with you!"
>
> Then Saul gave David his own armor—a bronze helmet and a coat of mail. David put it on, strapped the sword over it, and took a step or two to see what it was like, for he had never worn such things before.
>
> "I can't go in these," he protested to Saul. "I'm not used to them." So David took them off again. He picked up five smooth stones from a stream and put them into his shepherd's bag. Then, armed only with his shepherd's staff and sling, he started across the valley to fight the Philistine.
>
> Goliath walked out toward David with his shield bearer ahead of him, sneering in contempt at this ruddy-faced

boy. "Am I a dog," he roared at David, "that you come at me with a stick?" And he cursed David by the names of his gods. "Come over here, and I'll give your flesh to the birds and wild animals!" Goliath yelled.

David replied to the Philistine, "You come to me with sword, spear, and javelin, but I come to you in the name of the LORD of Heaven's Armies—the God of the armies of Israel, whom you have defied. Today the LORD will conquer you, and I will kill you and cut off your head. And then I will give the dead bodies of your men to the birds and wild animals, and the whole world will know that there is a God in Israel! And everyone assembled here will know that the LORD rescues his people, but not with sword and spear. This is the LORD's battle, and he will give you to us!"

As Goliath moved closer to attack, David quickly ran out to meet him. Reaching into his shepherd's bag and taking out a stone, he hurled it with his sling and hit the Philistine in the forehead. The stone sank in, and Goliath stumbled and fell face down on the ground.

So David triumphed over the Philistine with only a sling and a stone, for he had no sword.

1 Sam. 17:32–50 NLT

Thankfully, the situations we find ourselves in today are not life and death, as so many of the people from the Bible encountered during their lifetimes. However, facing a bully is undeniably frightening, and we can learn a lot from David and how he trusted in the Lord to see him through a standoff with Goliath. Look back at the passage for a minute, and let's unpack it a bit further.

David was a shepherd boy. He was young and inexperienced. Goliath was an elite warrior—a man who had been trained for battle since he was just a boy himself. The Bible tells us that Goliath's armor alone weighed more than a hundred pounds! All David felt comfortable using was his sling. King Saul and the rest of the Israelites must have been fearful for David's safety and well-being, as well as their own. Can you imagine? They probably thought poor David was heading off to be pummeled, and then they would still be forced into slavery! Yet what happened? David remained steadfast in his belief that God would protect and equip him. God did just that! In very unfavorable circumstances, David defeated the fierce soldier, Goliath, with only a smooth river rock and his sling.

Think of a time when you faced a bully of your own. When I was in the sixth grade, there was one girl in particular who did not care for me at all. She seemed to spend her days thinking of ways to embarrass me at school and always in front of other people. It was so bad at one point that I was getting stomach cramps before school every day. My parents tried to help, but they were not with me during the day. I felt alone, because none of my other friends had the courage to stand up to this particular mean girl in our class. We were all unsure what I did to deserve her wrath, but they did not want to be the target of her insults, either.

Look back at Matthew 5:43–48 from earlier in this chapter. I have provided the passage from another translation below.

> *You have heard the law that says, 'Love your neighbor' and hate your enemy. But I say, love your enemies! Pray for those who persecute you! In that way, you will be acting as true children of your Father in heaven. For he gives his sunlight to both the evil and the good, and he sends rain on the just and the unjust alike. If you love only those who love you, what reward is there for that? Even corrupt tax collectors do that much. If you are kind only to your friends, how are you different from anyone else? Even*

TRY A DIFFERENT TRANSLATION!

Moms and daughters, you may have noticed I use several different Bible translations throughout the Bible study. This is intentional. I grew up reading the King James Version, which is beautiful, but we no longer speak that way. For me, that particular translation is sometimes difficult to understand. During Bible study class, I encourage moms and daughters to look up passages using different translations. One may resonate better in your spirit and be easier to understand. There is no right or wrong translation, and I often work from at least three different Bible translations when I am looking up a passage.

There is no need to purchase several different translations, either. There are plenty of free resources available to you. Here are a few of my online favorites:

- ▸ biblegateway.com
- ▸ biblehub.com
- ▸ biblestudytools.com

pagans do that. But you are to be perfect, even as your
Father in heaven is perfect.

Matt. 5:43–48 NLT

Well, friends. I gave this a try with my mean girl. I prayed and prayed that God would change this person's heart and help me learn how to stand up for myself. Of course, I had to continue going to school. But instead of hanging my head and avoiding this particular girl, I tried to be nice to her. When she made fun of me, as she often did, this was not easy to do. I did it, though. I offered words of encouragement when I saw her struggling in class with her schoolwork. I smiled and said hello as I passed her at lunch—even if she responded unkindly or not at all.

Eventually, I noticed a change in her behavior. She no longer singled me out with embarrassing pranks in the hallway or lunchroom. She even occasionally said hello to me. While we never became good friends, I did later learn my mean girl was dealing with her parents' divorce. Did that make her choice to be mean to others okay? Absolutely not. However, it did help me understand her unhappiness a little better.

We do not always know what is going on in the lives of others around us. That is okay. We do not need to know those details. What is helpful to remember, though, is that we are all coping with something in our personal lives. God created each and every one of us out of love and with a loving purpose. When we feel oppressed by the hurtful actions of others, it can be tough to think of positive reasons that they are in our lives. However, I firmly believe God does not waste any experience—good or bad. He can be using your faith and courage to plant a seed in the heart of another—perhaps with the very person who has bullied you.

Be strong and courageous. Do not be afraid or terrified
because of them, for the LORD your God goes with you;
he will never leave you nor forsake you.

Deut. 31:6 (NIV)

If you are dealing with your own mean girl, take heart. You are not alone. This is a season you will weather as the girl of grace you are. Keep talking with your parents, but more importantly, keep talking to God. He will never leave you nor forsake you.

If you ever feel that you are physically in danger or that you are being verbally or emotionally abused, immediately tell your parents or another adult you trust. God places these people in your life to help navigate situations that you may not be able to handle alone, and these are lifelines you should use. Sometimes, a situation is beyond your ability to manage alone, so reach out to an adult you trust who can help you through your conflict. They can help equip you with additional tools and provide more resources you may need to resolve the bullying behavior. Asking for help is not a sign of weakness, girls. It takes courage to reach for help when you really need it, so do not be afraid to ask your parents or another trusted adult for backup.

 ## girl of grace HEarT CHECK

♥ What does being a bully mean to you? List a few characteristics that a mean girl or bully may have.

▶

▶

▶

♥ Talk with Mom about an experience you have had with a bully or mean girl at school. Have you resolved the conflict?

♥ Mom, talk with your daughter about how we encounter bullies throughout our lives. Share examples of ways you have coped with a mean girl or bully in your life.

♥ How can praying and living out Matthew 5:43–48 be life-changing—for ourselves as well as the people we interact with?

♥ Talk with Mom and use the space below to list what you think could be the motivations behind mean behaviors.

  ▶

  ▶

  ▶

♥ If you are struggling with a bully in your life, take time with Mom to pray for that person right now. Then pray for this person by name aloud every day this week with Mom.

an activity for mom and me: LeTTer To a meAN GirL

Girls are designed so differently than boys. This is not a shock. If you have spent any time with the opposite gender, then you know we communicate very differently. Girls are supposed to be sugar and spice and everything nice, right? Well, not always!

Sometimes, our actions hurt rather than nurture—and we have the ability to do this with our words, with our facial expressions—even with simple body language. Chances are pretty good that by the time you have reached elementary school, you have already had your first encounter with a mean girl. What is more, whether we want to admit it or not, we have probably taken our turn as the mean girl a time or two!

This week's Mom and Me activity involves writing a letter to a mean girl. You heard me correctly, ladies. If you are coping with a mean girl at school, on one of your sports teams, or in some other way—take some time this week to talk about it with Mom. Mom, this activity is for you as well. This is a great opportunity to talk with your tween darling about the fact that we continue to encounter bullies and mean girls even as adults.

We are going to do our best to live out Matthew 5:43–48. After you have talked with one another about your experiences, draft a letter to

Taking a Stand

Bullying behaviors can manifest in multiple ways. Sometimes the behavior is physical, and sometimes it is verbal. Bullying can take place in person, but these types of behaviors can also happen through email, social media, and cell phones. Regardless of how and where it happens, bullying is a problem.

Whether you have been on the receiving end or the distributing end of bullying behavior, you always have a choice how you react to these types of situations. We have already discussed potential ways to cope when you are the target of bullying. Have you ever witnessed the bullying of another person and felt helpless to do something about it?

Your circle of grace is filled with people God may reach through you and who God may use to connect with you. When you see a classmate getting picked on at school, is it your place to help? It absolutely can be your place. Did you know more than half of bullying situations (57 percent) stop when a your mean girl. The purpose of this letter is to be positive and reaffirming. It can be completely anonymous if you like—because the most important part of the activity comes next. After you have prayerfully written a letter to your mean girl, deliver it. Send it via snail mail, or leave it on her doorstep. The method of delivery is entirely up to you.

This activity is not meant to be easy. Living as Christians in a broken world is not simple! It can be downright scary. However, this activity is a good reminder that God has called us to love one another as he loves us. We rarely grow when we are comfortable, so feel your spirit stretch this week as you take time to reaffirm someone who has been mean to you.

Moms, please use your discernment here. If delivering a letter will exacerbate the situation between your daughter and her mean girl, do not send. A few moms in the pilot group for this study worked with their daughters to write their letters, and then they prayed over the letter and the girls as the letter was destroyed. One mom and daughter team even made s'mores over the fire afterward to celebrate giving the situation over to God. If you decide not to deliver your letter, brainstorm with your daughter other ways she can live out Matthew 5:43–48 with the person who is taunting her.

peer intervenes on behalf of the student being bullied?[1] Often, students or peers are aware of bullying conflicts before adults in the school. How should we empower our children to safely intervene?

The Bible gives us instruction for standing up for a friend. "This is My commandment, that you love one another, just as I have loved you. Greater love has no one than this, that one lay down his life for his friends" (John 15:12–13 NASB). Standing up for the victim of bullying may look as simple as sitting next to him or her at lunch, or walking with that person in the hallway at school. Perhaps standing up for someone comes in the form of a note that tells the recipient how special he or she is. How would you want someone to stand up for you?

The story of the Good Samaritan provides another excellent example for us. Take a look.

---

[1]D. Lynn Hawkins, Debra J. Pepler, and Wendy M. Craig, "Naturalistic Observations of Peer Interventions in Bullying," *Social Development* 10.4 (2001): 512–527, doi: 10.1111/1467-9507.00178.

Just then a religion scholar stood up with a question to test Jesus. "Teacher, what do I need to do to get eternal life?"

He answered, "What's written in God's Law? How do you interpret it?"

He said, "That you love the Lord your God with all your passion and prayer and muscle and intelligence—and that you love your neighbor as well as you do yourself."

"Good answer!" said Jesus. "Do it and you'll live."

Looking for a loophole, he asked, "And just how would you define 'neighbor'?"

Jesus answered by telling a story. "There was once a man traveling from Jerusalem to Jericho. On the way he was attacked by robbers. They took his clothes, beat him up, and went off leaving him half-dead. Luckily, a priest was on his way down the same road, but when he saw him he angled across to the other side. Then a Levite religious man showed up; he also avoided the injured man.

"A Samaritan traveling the road came on him. When he saw the man's condition, his heart went out to him. He gave him first aid, disinfecting and bandaging his wounds. Then he lifted him onto his donkey, led him to an inn, and made him comfortable. In the morning he took out two silver coins and gave them to the innkeeper, saying, 'Take good care of him. If it costs any more, put it on my bill—I'll pay you on my way back.'

"What do you think? Which of the three became a neighbor to the man attacked by robbers?"

"The one who treated him kindly," the religion scholar responded.

Jesus said, "Go and do the same."

Luke 10:25–37 The Message

As long as you are trying to lift up others around you—regardless of their social status and your role in the scenario at hand—you are following the instruction given us in passages such as those found in the parable of the Good Samaritan, Matthew 5:43–48, and John 15:12–13. These types of encounters are often uncomfortable, and we cannot always see God's hand at work—but he is ever-present and working through you! Walk faithfully and trust the Holy Spirit to guide you.

girl of grace HEarT CHECK

♥ If you have had a chance to complete the activity for Mom and Me this week, talk with Mom about how this experience made you feel.

♥ If you delivered your letter, how was it received?

♥ What obstacles keep you from more fully living out Matthew 5:43–48?

♥ Read 2 Timothy 1:7. Talk with Mom about what this passage means to you and write your thoughts below.

♥ We have all played the role of bully at one time or another, whether we realize it or not. Why do we sometimes feel like being mean?

♥ How do we change this kind of behavior?

♥ Brainstorm with Mom on ways you can make a positive difference when you encounter a situation where someone else is being bullied. Write your ideas in the space below.

▸

▸

▸

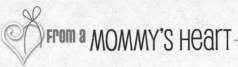

FROM A MOMMY'S HEART

Moms, bullying is a tough topic for so many reasons. There is no perfect solution to bullying, and technology has taken this type of behavior to another dreaded level. The purpose of the Bible studies I have written is to serve as a catalyst for moms and their tween daughters to read the Word of God together and openly communicate about what is happening in their day-to-day lives. The questions included are designed to be conversation starters so moms and daughters are talking together through what can be pretty tough topics and life experiences.

The tween years are exciting and frightening at the same time. These sweet girls are literally caught between their childhood and teenage years. Their hearts are still open to the wisdom of our mommy words, and my prayer is that each of us uses this preciously short time to reaffirm with our girls that their moms are present and supportive—always.

While I have chosen to focus this bullying topic on the positive choices we can make in these types of situations, I am readily aware some scenarios cannot be resolved without parental or other adult intervention. In no way am I advocating your child should turn the other cheek and show kindness if she is being physically or emotionally bullied. God calls us to be loving and forgiving of one another, but he does not call us to be doormats. Through these extreme cases of bullying, praying is always part of the solution. However, I am not suggesting it is the only solution.

God entrusted these special creatures into our care, and it is our responsibility to serve as their advocates, especially in circumstances where their emotional or physical health is being compromised. Use prayer and your parental discretion to determine where you personally draw the line.

I have already shared my oldest daughter's experience with bullying. She got into my car nearly every day of her kindergarten year in tears over something one particular classmate had said or done. As her mom, I wanted to call the parent of this other child and stand up for my daughter—but my husband and I knew this was not the answer. While we did talk with my daughter's teacher, we chose to pray for this other student and coach our own daughter on ways to stand up for herself.

Our daughter was in class a few years later with this same student. Again, the school year started with tears and anger over how our daughter was being physically and emotionally bullied. My husband and I once again spoke with our daughter's teacher and brainstormed strategies on how to resolve the situation peacefully and positively. We learned the other student was not actively trying to bully our daughter. This other student just liked being first—at everything. My daughter figured out what motivated the behavior of this other student and modified her own choices. The result was a smoother school year and almost no tears from bullying.

Again, I want to stress the goal for these Bible studies is to help create transparent and regular communication with our daughters. I do not ever want my girls to feel like what they have to say and how they feel is not important to their dad and me. No, I am not a psychology expert. I am a mom who loves her children more than words can ever adequately convey. As parents, we need to encourage and pray for one another as we are all swimming through this broken world trying to teach our kids that God is always present, that their parents will always love and support them, and that they always have a choice.

CHAPTER 7

SOCIAL VS.
"UN"SOCIAL MEDIA

"In the same way, let your light shine before men, so that they may see your good works and give glory to your Father in heaven."

Matt. 5:16 HCSB

ONE OF THE DEFINING PHENOMENA reshaping society, as we know it, is our world-wide accessibility to the Internet. Social media is an offspring of the Internet that comes in many forms, including blogs, forums, photo-sharing platforms, social gaming, chat apps, and social networks. In this chapter, we are going to focus on the latter. Did you know that more than 2.2 billion people have social media accounts (according to Social Media Today)? That is nearly 30 percent of the world's population. Social Media Today also reports that Facebook adds half a million new users every single day—that is six new profiles every second. Wow.

Mamas and daughters, think on this for a second. What this shows us, girls, is that social media is not going anywhere. I grew up in a time when if you wanted to be social, you went outside to play. We had telephones that connected to the wall with corded handsets. If you were really cool, your parents provided three-way calling so a whopping three people could talk on the same line at once. It was fancy stuff!

Moms, the reality is our kids are growing up in a culture where technology and social media are second nature. My daughters can operate my iPhone better than I can, and it seems intuitive. There are many blessings that come with this kind of technology and connectivity, but there are also quite a few dangers lurking in the virtual realm.

The Impact of Virtual Connectivity

In a world that is more connected than ever, it seems appropriate to have a conversation about the effects of social media on our circles of grace. When we talk about social media in this Bible study, we are referring to applications like Facebook, Google+, Instagram, LinkedIn, Pinterest, Snapchat, Twitter, and so on.

Social media feeds our desire to feel connected. Undeniably, we place a heavy emphasis on feeling connected through one or more of these tools. How many of these applications do you have on your phone or computer? How often do you check them each day?

If we were to compare our society with a biblical civilization, we could likely name numerous differences between the two. Technology, science, medicine, modern-day conveniences, and how we communicate are just a few of the examples that would likely pop up in our comparison. However, two things always hold true: God's Word and human nature. Just because the Bible was written long ago does not mean it loses relevancy in our lives today. Also, the social dilemmas that we experience today are vividly apparent in God's Word. Why? In spite of our modern advances, human nature remains the same.

In this chapter, we are going to explore four ways in which social media can impact the relationships in your circles of grace. Let's take a peek at the first one.

What did we talk about in Chapter Four? Yep, we dug into the topic of gossip. With social media, we have been given a tool that enables us to create and spread gossip faster than ever before. The Bible says nothing directly about social media, but there is plenty about the negative impact of gossip. "Do not spread slanderous gossip among your people. Do not stand idly by when your neighbor's life is threatened. I am the LORD" (Lev. 19:16 NLT).

Even though the Scriptures were finalized approximately two thousand years before social media was invented, the Bible is full of instruction that can guide how we use these tools. Think about how quickly computers and mobile devices allow us to connect with others. We are also easily connected with so many more people than before we used computers and cell phones. It takes literally seconds to post a simple something about your day or to share some juicy tidbit of news, and then bam! Your virtual voice can be heard literally around the globe.

People you do not even know have access to what you share online (and perhaps there are folks who should not be part of your circle). Thinking about social media from this perspective might motivate girls of grace to be more careful about what they say or the pictures they post.

Remember, girls. Words have power. Social media sites are often used as vehicles to spread gossip or bully others, because social media sites deceptively enable us to think we can say things we might not normally say to someone's face. Whether through the power of anonymity or the fact that we cannot see the reaction our words cause, social media gives a unique sense of freedom to say what we want and when we want without consequences.

This is perhaps the greatest fallacy of social media. All actions have consequences, even when you do not see them unfold before your eyes. When you spread gossip or use social media to make someone feel anything other than loved and worthy, you are allowing the enemy to use you as an instrument of hurt.

> *There is more hope for a fool than for someone who speaks without thinking.*
> Prov. 29:20 NLT

Remember, human nature remains the same, but this does not mean God cannot use social media for a positive purpose. In a society that encourages us to think much about ourselves and places a high value on the opinion of others, dare to be different. Just because you are young does not mean you are unable to lead. "Let no one despise you for your youth, but set the believers an example in speech, in conduct, in love, in faith, in purity" (1 Tim. 4:12 ESV).

Set a positive example for others and be a positive instrument of peer pressure within your circles of grace by choosing to use social media as a place to love your neighbor. Because what does God ask us to do above all else? He calls us to know him and to make him known. In this instance, your neighbors are those other voices all around the globe. If you are using social media to further God's calling in this way, you are living out 1 Timothy 4:12.

Another impact social media may have on your circles of grace is the amount of time you spend on these websites. Social media websites can be a super-powered vacuum on your time. Girls, I enjoy Pinterest so much. I can easily spend an hour perusing wonderful ideas without realizing how long I have been on the site. Last year during Lent, I gave up social media for forty days. Initially, I found myself opening my phone randomly (at a stoplight, while waiting for my girls to finish an assignment, or just sitting with my prince charming on the couch). How eye-opening to realize that I was wasting so much precious time browsing through various social media outlets. By the end of those forty days, I was relishing my newfound freedom.

How much time do you spend on social media sites each day? Could the time you spend on those sites be better utilized through other activities such as spending time with God or your family, praying, or finishing that school assignment you have been putting off? I readily admit how enticing the temptation of social media can be, and to be honest, I am not suggesting the use of social media is wrong. The more time you spend on these sites, however, the more exposure your heart has to worldly standards. Beautiful means looking like . . . I had no idea those girls from school were . . . I wonder if I could . . .

Your eyes have a direct line to your heart, and with God's help and discernment, it is your job to guard it. "Your eye is a like lamp that provides light for your body. When your eye is healthy, your whole body is filled with light. But when it is unhealthy, your body is filled with darkness" (Luke 11:34 NLT).

girl of grace HEarT CHECK

♥ Does the content you view on social media sites affect the way you see yourself or the way you see others?

♥ If you answered yes to the question above, talk with Mom about how and why.

♥ Look up Romans 12:2 and write it in the space below.

♥ Read the following passage.

Their idols are merely things of silver and gold,
shaped by human hands.
They have mouths but cannot speak,
and eyes but cannot see.
They have ears but cannot hear,
and noses but cannot smell.
They have hands but cannot feel,
and feet but cannot walk,
and throats but cannot make a sound.
And those who make idols are just like them,
as are all who trust in them.

Ps. 115:4–8 NLT

After reading through the psalm, write examples of what could be worldly idols below.

▶

▶

▶

▶

♥ Talk with Mom about what Romans 12:2 means to you and how it might be used to help us remember not to allow social media to become an idol.

♥ How are you guarding your heart when using social media? Brainstorm with Mom some other ways you can be doing this.

♥ Read Matthew 5:16. Do people see the light of Christ in you based on what you share through social media outlets?

an activity for mom and me: SPReaDING LOVe

Because we live in a world so connected through social media outlets, this week's Mom and Me activity encourages us to distinguish between being connected and connectedness.

If possible, take a break from social media this week and spend that time instead making cards for friends and neighbors. This week is about connecting the old-fashioned way! Remember, your neighbor is anyone, not just the people who may live next door to you. You may absolutely purchase premade cards, but please feel empowered to make them from scratch! A lot can be done with a small piece of card stock or construction paper. You may even get creative with the shape and cut them into hearts or some other fun design. Decorate your cards with pictures, stickers, or (my personal favorite) glitter!

Perhaps you know someone who could use words of affirmation this week. Instead of posting on their social media page, deliver a card in person or through the mail. *Snail* mail, not email! Think about how excited you are when you receive a card in the mail versus a text on your phone. You may be surprised how delighted the recipients of your cards feel, and it may set off a positive chain reaction as they in turn spread the love!

saving Face

What is more fun? Would you rather spend time browsing and posting to social media sites, or would you prefer hanging out with your friends in person? Hopefully you chose kicking back with your gal pals. Our Mom and Me activity posed an important question that I hope you discussed. What is the difference between being connected and connectedness?

Social media sites certainly enable us to be connected, and sometimes this connection is extremely positive. For example, Facebook enables me to stay in touch with friends and family who live far away. These are people whom I love dearly, and without the help of social media, I would not be able to connect with them on a regular basis. However, the third way in which social media can impact our circles is the direct effect these tools have on our face-to-face interactions. This could be said for more than social media, as well. While we are connected through social media and online devices, are we really experiencing connectedness?

My oldest daughter recently sent me a text while she was in her bedroom to ask a question about homework. I was sitting on the couch in our living room at the time. Uh, no. Her preferred mode of communication at the time gave us an opportunity to talk about face-to-face interaction and the scary dependence we sometimes have on electronic devices when it comes to our ability to connect. Mamas, have you ever sent a coworker an email instead of getting up and walking down to his or her office, simply because it was faster and easier? I have been guilty of this on a number of occasions. Connectedness comes from in-person interactions, not online exchanges.

Remember those days of talking on the phone with our friends for hours? Or better yet, how much more fun is it to sit and giggle with your friends in person? Modern technology provides an alternate form of communication and enables us to stay in touch with people we otherwise might not, but it by no means should be our only or primary form of communication. How exhausting to think about limiting what you want to say to 140 characters!

At the very heart of who God is, there is community and connectedness. We experience this through the Trinity: the Father, the Son, and the Holy Spirit. God is community, and he created humans in his likeness. Therefore, at the very core of who we are as God's image bearers, God designed us to experience connectedness with him and with one another. "Beloved, let us love one another, for love is from God, and whoever loves has been born of God and knows God" (1 John 4:7 ESV).

Our relationships can become superficial if we primarily interact with people online and not in person. Think about how we use social media. All of these interactions are done in isolation, separate from human contact. God created us for community and connectedness, not for superficial relationships. Communication is often more meaningful when it happens face-to-face.

> *Though I have much to write to you, I would rather not use paper and ink. Instead I hope to come to you and talk face to face, so that our joy may be complete.*
>
> 2 John 1:12 ESV

Perhaps you use social media to promote face-to-face connectivity, such as a small group study or church concert. Again, the lesson here is not that we should be against social media. On the contrary, God can use these tools to help us come together in a way we may not have before. When we provide space and opportunities for community and connectedness, God can bless your circle in a big way.

The fourth and final potential impact of social media that we will discuss is the effect on your future. When you post a comment, status, photo, or something similar to social media sites, your virtual imprint will last long into your future. Universities and employers often use social media sites to screen potential applicants. The ramifications of any questionable content, even if it is in the past, can come back to haunt you. As a rule of thumb, it is safe to assume that everything written through social media outlets is permanent and viewable by everyone.

With that being said, social media outlets can be a vast mission field for Christians. We keep talking about the power of words and positive peer pressure. Through social media, Christians have the ability to influence countless neighbors. Instead of spreading gossip, we can choose to post encouraging and affirming words that God may use to plant seeds for others' spiritual guidance.

> *Let us think of ways to motivate one another to acts of love and good works. And let us not neglect our meeting together, as some people do, but encourage one another, especially now that the day of his return is drawing near.*
>
> Heb. 10:24–25 NLT

Let's wrap up our discussion of social media by discussing some helpful questions to think through before posting to one of these sites. Before clicking *Post* or *Tweet*, think:

Do I mind if my parents see this?
Do I mind if my pastor sees this?
Is what I am posting true?
Is what I am posting my story to tell?
Is what I am posting glorifying God?

Think before you post, girls. Use discretion when adding friends or fans. Social media is not about the number of friends you have nor the number of likes your posts receive. Not everyone online has honorable intentions, so it is important to keep mom and dad informed of any activity that makes you uncomfortable.

At the end of the day, rely on the Holy Spirit to guide your actions, and trust your parents to set healthy parameters for social media usage. It is your job to guard your heart, but God has entrusted you to your parents for a wonderful purpose. It is their job to guard your heart as well.

 ## girl of grace HeArT CHeCK

💜 Do you value social media interactions more than real-life relationships?

💜 Look up James 3:10 and write it in the space below.

💜 Do your words affirm or destroy?

♥ Read 1 Corinthians 15:33. Talk with Mom about what this passage means.

♥ Are there relationships in your circle through social media outlets that are unhealthy?

♥ Do you spend as much time with God as you spend on social media sites?

♥ Brainstorm with Mom at least three ways you can make a change if your priorities need a little rearranging.

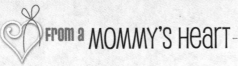

from a MOMMY'S HearT

When I sat down to write this chapter and prayed through the message on social media, a childhood song kept coming to mind—"Oh, Be Careful Little Eyes." We talked about it in Chapter Two.

I have to be honest, mamas. We live in a world that terrifies me. The brokenness of our world is blatantly apparent on the news, in magazines, and especially through outlets such as social media sites. We are bombarded daily with images and words that tell us who we are, what we should believe, and why.

The little girl in me wants to crawl into my Father's lap and simply let him protect his little lamb. As mamas, though, we have the earthly job as shepherds for the babies that have been entrusted into our care. Ladies, there is a lion in our camp! Satan is cunning and tireless in his pursuit of our children. We must be vigilant to guard their hearts as they are learning how to defend themselves on their own. Part of our role is equipping our daughters with the tools they need to fight an enemy that they cannot always see. He slips by, often undetected, through words and images that plant dark seeds of untruth in their hearts.

God has already defeated him. We know how this story ends. However, until the day that Jesus returns, the battle on earth continues. I am not being dramatic, friends. This war is real, and our children must be taught how to guard their hearts while living out the call to know God and to make him known. How do we do this? My husband and I struggle daily. God has given us the best instruction manual possible, but we are human. We make mistakes. We sometimes set poor examples for our children. This is especially true of my time spent on Pinterest and Facebook.

Another potentially harmful side effect of social media is the impact on our sense of self. Social media is a huge marketing tool, and as a writer, my focus is sometimes on the depth of reach in terms of readership.

God recently freed my spirit from this stranglehold. It was not narcissism in the sense that I must feel so important. However, I was constantly concerned with the number of likes my author page collected. When my husband and I agreed to allow my oldest to join Pinterest, she immediately stressed over the number of followers and likes she had. This was eye-opening to me.

Social media outlets are not inherently wrong. On the contrary, I believe God can use these tools for some pretty amazing kingdom work. However, there is an inherent danger in self-oriented sites that encourage us to promote ourselves and draw attention to words and life events that perhaps we should not. The truth is the number of friends, followers, fans, or likes does not matter. If we are using social media outlets in a way that glorifies God, then we can trust that he is sowing seeds where they should be sowed.

Part of our job as parents is to hold our sweet cherubs accountable while they are still under our wings. Yet God also uses our children to hold us accountable, and this is so much bigger than social media. Has your child ever parroted your words back to you? It happens in my house with regular occurrence, and my girls are honestly not being sassy. It is a simple reminder of two very important things: we are all human, and we all need Jesus.

CHapter 8

Developing
accountability

*God didn't set us up for an angry rejection but for salvation by
our Master, Jesus Christ. He died for us, a death that triggered life.
Whether we're awake with the living or asleep with the dead, we're
alive with him! So speak encouraging words to one another. Build
up hope so you'll all be together in this, no one left out, no one left
behind. I know you're already doing this; just keep on doing it.*

1 Thess. 5:9–11 *The Message*

remember at the beginning of our study we talked about celebrating the beauty of *you*? Every single one of us is fearfully and wonderfully made! We also discussed that you reside deep in the heart of your circle of grace, which is comprised of all the relationships in your life. At the heart of you is God. Your relationship with God is the foundation for your own circle of grace. If you keep Christ at the center of your heart, you are laying a solid foundation for Christ-centered relationships with others.

Your circle reflects the people (or relationships) who surround you in life—whether by choice or circumstance. God built us for connectedness and community, so we naturally seek relationships with others. Over the course of the last seven weeks, we have explored some of the dynamics we encounter through our relationships with other people. Regardless of our background or circumstance, every one of us can relate in some way to stressors in family relationships, friendship highs and lows, mean girls, and the attraction to social media. My hope is that through the course of this study, you have spent time in the Word of God and engaged in meaningful mother and daughter conversations about the impact each of these has on your own circles of grace.

The importance of checks and Balances

To finish out our eight-week study, we are going to spend the last chapter in a discussion about accountability. What is accountability? *Merriam-Webster* defines accountability as "an obligation or willingness to accept responsibility or to account for one's actions." So think of accountability as a sort of "checks and balances" system for our circles of grace that helps keep our relationships healthy.

We are all held accountable in some way. For example, your parents hold you accountable when you break a rule at home or forget to complete your chores around the house. Your teachers hold you accountable for turning in assignments and completing your work with integrity. As citizens, there are laws to obey and if we fail to obey them, we may suffer consequences set by the officials who hold us accountable. Accountability is simply being responsible for one's actions, and sometimes we need help being held accountable.

This is important, girls. Every single one of us needs accountability, so let's talk about what that looks like within our circles of grace.

Who Holds Us accountable?

The first and most important source of our accountability is God. Who better to hold us responsible for our actions than the loving Creator who so carefully crafted us? Jesus spoke often about accountability. Look what he says in Matthew: "And I tell you this, you must give an account on judgment day for every idle word you speak" (Matt. 12:36 NLT).

Friends, it is tough to take responsibility for our actions and words. Think back to Adam and Eve when they took that infamous bite of the fruit that would open their eyes to the knowledge of good and evil. Neither wanted to acknowledge their role in what happened. Adam blamed Eve, and Eve blamed the serpent. God showed grace and forgiveness, but he also held Adam and Eve responsible for their choices. As Christians, we are saved through God's grace, yet we are still full of sin. We all struggle with thoughts, actions, and choices that can diminish our relationships with God. Remember, God created us out of love for love and for community. He longs for a relationship with all of his children.

However, do not confuse accountability with judgment, which is reserved for God and God alone. "This is the message I proclaim—that the day is coming when God, through Christ Jesus, will judge everyone's secret life" (Rom. 2:16 NLT). What else have we talked through again and again? Above all else,

God calls us to know him and to make him known. While we were built for community, God did not grant us permission to judge one another. He does, however, ask that we hold one another *accountable*. "Preach the word; be prepared in season and out of season; correct, rebuke and encourage—with great patience and careful instruction" (2 Tim. 4:2 NIV). Pay special attention to that last part—with great patience and careful instruction. The truth may not always be easy to hear, but it must still be spoken. However, the truth must be accompanied by love.

One of the primary relationships God uses to hold us accountable is family. Who better to speak truth in love than the special people God selected as your family? Part of a parent's role is to teach, correct, and encourage our children. Part of a child's role is to take instruction, encouragement, and correction. How wonderful and wise that God allows us to learn from one another—no matter what our age may be.

God often provides opportunities for my children to hold me accountable for my actions. For example, remember how I mentioned in Chapter One the self-deprecating comments I sometimes make about myself? Mamas are not immune to the awful and deceitful fallacies that society spews into our hearts about the meaning of true beauty. While I am ever careful to speak words of affirmation into my children's spirits, I sometimes forget to speak those affirming words into my own. When this happens, God uses my girls to remind me that I am beautiful in his eyes and that he does not make mistakes.

My children are not judging me in these instances of self-doubt. Rather, my girls lovingly hold me accountable. They are speaking truth in love. This truth-telling comes from their hearts.

Contrary to any preconceived notions, accountability is not about confrontation. We may, at times, need to be confronted and to confront another, but accountability is more about challenging one another to grow in Christ and remember who God has called us to be.

 girl of grace HEART CHECK

♥ Look up 1 Corinthians 3:23 and write it down in the space below.

♥ Talk with Mom about what this means and how this Scripture relates to accountability.

♥ Why do we need accountability?

♥ How is God's role in our accountability different from that of our family members?

♥ What is the difference between judging people for their actions versus holding them accountable?

an activity for mom and me: a COVENANT OF LOVE

As our eight-week study draws to a close, I encourage you to spend this week drafting a mother and daughter "Covenant of Accountability." In short, put down on paper how you plan to live out the following passage together going forward.

> *Let us hold tightly without wavering to the hope*
> *we affirm, for God can be trusted to keep his*
> *promise. Let us think of ways to motivate one*
> *another to acts of love and good works. And let*
> *us not neglect our meeting together, as some*
> *people do, but encourage one another, especially*
> *now that the day of his return is drawing near.*
>
> Heb. 10:23–25 NLT

Before you begin, take time to pray and ask God to place ideas on your heart for what to include in your promise to one another. Your covenant can be as simple or as elaborate as you like. Here are a few examples of things you may want to include:

- ♥ Commitment to meeting weekly—just mom and daughter—to check in, share, and pray together.
- ♥ Commit to serving together in your community. (Perhaps there is a mission that is near and dear to both of you!)
- ♥ Brainstorm ways you can consistently encourage one another and others in your circles of grace (a handwritten note of encouragement, a home-cooked meal, etc.).

After your covenant is drafted, pray over your promise as mother and daughter. Make a copy so each of you has one. Place the covenant in your Bibles and revisit it in a few months to hold yourselves accountable.

accountability from the Heart

Accountability enables us to share our lives with one another in a deep, introspective way. This allows for deeper, more meaningful connections. Upon reflection on your circle, you may find many of your relationships in life tend to be casual and superficial. Yet we need deep connections. Let's repeat our mantra again. God created us for community. Girls, imprint this truth on your hearts!

Another source God utilizes to hold his wayward children accountable is the friends we choose for ourselves. As we have discussed, these relationships tend to be some of the brightest blessings God gives us. Our trusted confidantes are those we typically want to call first when we have fun news to share or want to lean on when we are feeling blue. We also tend to care a great deal about what these people think. God is so smart, friends. Sometimes I swear my children are deaf to the frequency of my voice. Yet, they are so in tune to their friends' voices. God often uses these relationships to reach our hearts when we need accountability.

Jesus's twelve disciples beautifully model for us what it means to hold friends accountable. This close-knit group of friends experienced and endured much during their time together. Sometimes they made poor choices. Yet they repeatedly extended forgiveness and grace to one another. Peter denied knowing Jesus when, some may argue, it counted most. He was afraid of what his relationship with Jesus would mean for his own future. He could feasibly have been put to death as well. This man had already shown great faith in the Son of Man, and you may remember Peter's faith when he walked on water with Jesus.

> *Immediately he made the disciples get into the boat and go before him to the other side, while he dismissed the crowds. And after he had dismissed the crowds, he went up on the mountain by himself to pray. When evening came, he was there alone, but the boat by this time was a long way from the land, beaten by the waves, for the wind was against them. And in the fourth watch of the night he came to them, walking on the sea. But when the disciples saw him walking on the sea, they were terrified, and said, "It is a ghost!" and they cried out in fear. But immediately Jesus spoke to them, saying, "Take heart; it is I. Do not be afraid." And Peter answered him, "Lord, if*

it is you, command me to come to you on the water." He
said, "Come." So Peter got out of the boat and walked
on the water and came to Jesus.

Matt. 14:22–29 ESV

Peter was a man of great faith, and the Bible tells us that he loved Jesus deeply. However, Peter, in his human brokenness, made mistakes (just like you and I). Jesus was truthful with Peter when he foretold that Peter would deny him. Goodness, can you imagine how awful Peter must have felt? Especially when what Jesus foretold came to pass. Jesus spoke truth, but he spoke truth with love. Peter had to face that truth and be accountable for his actions. Do you think the other disciples and Jesus wrote Peter off because of his poor choice? Even though Peter felt terrible and wanted to return to his life as a fisherman, his friends did not allow him to throw in the towel. There was no judgment, simply forgiveness and grace along with a loving reminder of Peter's commitment to discipleship. Girls, this is friendly accountability at its finest.

My brothers and sisters, if one of you should wander
from the truth and someone should bring that person
back, remember this: Whoever turns a sinner from the
error of their way will save them from death and cover
over a multitude of sins.

James 5:19–20 (NIV)

Having other people around whom you can trust and get to know more deeply will enable you to know yourself—your *true* self—more deeply. Rather than buying into the misbelief of who you should be according to ever-changing worldly standards, you will be able to embrace your authentic identity as God's image bearer and the girl of grace he has designed you to be.

God empowers each of us to hold ourselves accountable. "Do not waste time arguing over godless ideas and old wives' tales. Instead, train yourself to be godly" (1 Tim. 4:7 NLT). I love this Scripture passage! Think about all the lies that the enemy hurls at us through society's contact lens every single day. Lies! Our instruction and truth come from the Bible. We can apply a very simple test to uncover a potential worldly untruth. If what we are hearing conflicts with God's Word, it is a fallacy (a mistaken belief or unsound argument).

For example, we live in a culture that encourages us to seek self-fulfillment through worldly pleasures such as money, objects, food, and entertainment.

Remember from the previous chapter: these are idols, friends, but the clever enemy would have us believe we are entitled to these things. Scripture tells us, "Blessed are those who hunger and thirst for righteousness, for they will be filled" (Matt. 5:6 NIV).

Because God created us, he always knows our hearts. We can trust he will never leave nor forsake us. Sometimes, though, our family and friends are not around to hold us accountable for our choices. The Bible teaches us to encourage, exhort, pray for, and correct one another in love and in Christ. It is helpful to remember this includes holding ourselves accountable for our actions and choices.

> *The older I get the less judgmental I feel and the more committed I am to telling the truth. Don't let anyone tell you they are the same. Judgment says: I know better than you; Truth telling says: I love you enough to share with you what I know. The heart behind it is what makes the difference. (God, please help me always be about the latter.)*
>
> Lisa Whittle, author of *I Want God* and *[W]hole*

We may be our own worst critics, easily relating to our friend Peter as he felt so defeated by his poor decisions. His accountability to himself was relentless and unforgiving. I love this quote from Lisa Whittle, and it is a gentle reminder to show love and grace to ourselves as well as others.

 girl of grace HEART CHECK

♥ Read James 5:19–20 again and write the Scripture below.

♥ Can you think of time when a friend held you accountable for a poor choice you made? Ask Mom to share, too.

♥ What about a time when you may have held a friend accountable for a choice he or she made? Talk about this with Mom.

♥ How did your friend react? Was it a positive or negative experience? Could you have done something differently?

♥ What does it mean to be your own worst critic?

♥ Do you relate to Peter? Why or why not?

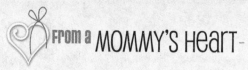

Whew . . . we made it to the end of this study, fellow mama. And yet, there is a lot of living ahead of us and for our daughters. I believe that a lot of living necessitates the need for accountability, making this a natural ending for this relational Bible study. My prayer is that you and your daughter engaged in deep and meaningful conversations about the relationships in your lives.

As mothers, the biggest aspect of accountability is presence. This looks like making time consistently to stare into your daughter's eyes. Listen, love, ask, be patient, pursue, speak truth—all of these actions play an important role for mamas who are accountable to God and who have authority in turn to hold their children accountable. We do this by aligning counsel and discipline with God's Word. Hopefully, this is exactly what you two have been doing throughout this Bible study.

God designed our daughters for worship. They will either worship the way of the world, or they will choose to worship God and his ways. Mamas, remember there is a lion in our camp! Satan longs for our daughters' worship. He longs for their attention. The enemy is clever, crafty, and patient. Undeniably, we see his presence in our day-to-day lives and in the would-be influence he wants to have over our children—and us.

God also designed us to be relational creatures. We were specially and carefully crafted to crave community. In a society that is more connected than ever by and through technology, this can lead to frightening scenarios. We talked in the last chapter about the difference between being connected versus connectedness. Mamas, being connected today does not mean what it did even ten years ago. Technology affords us ever-evolving ways to be in touch, yet at the same time, we find ourselves disconnected from face-to-face encounters. The dynamics of how we connect with others and develop relationships change almost as quickly as the development of new social media apps, and being connected through these trendy and fancy modes of communication seldom allows us to see others authentically. Frightening, right?

So how do you address these potentially scary situations? Be present. This accountability holds true for our daughters as well, but mamas, is it our responsibility to ensure our presence is felt no matter what the season of our children's lives. This does not look like stifling conversations and nagging. Be transparent with your accountability. She may not always act appreciative of your presence, but your daughter will be thankful for it just the same.

Lastly, hold one another accountable through prayer. Jesus said, "Where two or more are gathered, there I am in the midst of them." There is power in prayer—spoken prayer. Remember the Lord literally spoke our world into being. Pray Scripture over your girls consistently and faithfully. Pray the armor of God over yourself and your family. I also believe in the importance of speaking words of affirmation and empowerment about our daughters' true identities. Even if our tween darlings roll their eyes and appear not to care, we are still speaking truth and life into their spirits, using the Sword of the Spirit to combat any lies the enemy would have them believe.

The Mom and Me activity this week is to draft a covenant between mother and daughter. Moms, I know we live in a busy world. So often, many of our lives are set to the rhythm of rush. Might I encourage you to slow down, pray, and prepare a covenant that you two may use as a tool for accountability? You may choose to check in weekly or monthly, but please do check in.

Time is precious and fleeting. As moms, perhaps no one understands this better than we do. I blinked, and my daughter started walking. I blinked again, and she started school. A few more blinks and now high school is here for my oldest daughter.

Our days are full of school and extracurricular activities. Our schedule probably looks something like yours—busy. Let us be empowered to hit pause with frequency so that we may not only be present, but also that we may enjoy the presence of our daughters while they are in our care. I will be praying for you, mama. May God bless you and yours mightily!

a JOINT BIBLE STUDY
FOR TWEEN GIRLS AND THEIR MOMS

Facilitator's guide

FACILITATORS, this guide has been prayerfully written to aid you in small group study. Your primary role as a small group leader is facilitating discussion at your meetings. For some, this opportunity is exciting and thrilling. For others, the task feels daunting. Regardless of your comfort level with leading small group study, my goal was to write a guide that would make facilitating a less intimidating task. Within the pages of this guide are discussion questions and small group activities to help moms and tween daughters unpack Scriptures more fully, digging deeper into the heart of the study.

At your first meeting, I recommend asking your small group members (moms and tween girls) to sign a covenant of confidentiality (see sample at the end of the Facilitator's Guide). This particular study is about building and sustaining Christ-centered relationships. Building relationships requires trust and vulnerability. In order to foster transparent discussion about the sensitive topics included in this study, all small group members should feel safe to share. Your small group covenants are also a great tool for confirming participants' commitment of time and attendance.

Format of the Study

This study is unique in that it is not broken down by daily reading and study. This is an eight-week-long class designed to facilitate joint Bible study and discussion between mothers and daughters. Each week, we will examine a topic related to relationship building and add layers to these discussions as moms and daughters dig deeper into the study. The study is full of relevant Scripture passages and conversation starters to get moms and daughters thinking and talking about how these excerpts from God's Word are still relevant for us today.

Walk through the eight-week outline and briefly touch on the topics of study. Moms and daughters may approach weekly study however it fits into their schedules. If they want to read a little bit each day, great! If it works better for them to consolidate into two days, excellent! This study is intentionally flexible.

Each week, moms and daughters will also have an optional activity.

Encourage class participants to do these activities if at all possible, as they relate to each week's theme and will be just plain fun! I am personally a visual learner, so hands-on activities have always better helped me wrap my brain around a concept. These weekly activities are age appropriate, fun, and a different approach from traditional study to help moms and their daughters discuss, connect, and learn about Scripture together.

For moms: Please make note of a special section for them in each week's study called "From a Mommy's Heart." This section is for moms' hearts only and is an opportunity to tie a parent-related topic to each week of study. These sections are designed to complement the discussions moms and daughters are already having and give moms an extra tidbit to noodle on and pray through during their week of study.

Facilitator's guide

week one

open each class time with prayer. During your first meeting, take the first ten to fifteen minutes to make introductions. Pick one of the following icebreakers (or use one of your own) so mothers and daughters are able to get better acquainted.

TOILET paper GAME

Take a roll of toilet paper and ask each person how many squares she wants, but don't tell her what they are for. Set a limit from five to ten. Count out the number of requested squares, and give them to the class attendee. Repeat until all the participants have the requested amount of toilet paper squares. After everyone has taken her tissue, ask each mom and daughter to share something about herself for every square of toilet paper she has taken.

GOD aND THE FAMILY BOND

Give each mom and daughter a list of questions you have made up ahead of time. Use your imagination to make a list of twenty or more preferential questions like, "Who is your favorite movie star?" or "What is your favorite book?" You can ask about colors, music, plays, TV shows, or hopes for the future. Place two columns next to each of the questions, one for the mother and one for the daughter. Ask each mom and daughter to write down her own favorite and what she thinks is her mother's or daughter's favorite. The pair goes over the list together. Talk about how God knows us better even than our own family.

aBCS OF Me

First, take a piece of paper and write your name vertically down the left side. Next, choose a word that starts with each letter of your name. The word should describe something about you. Write those words horizontally across the paper, using the letters of your name as the first letter of each descriptive word. After you have listed your words, draw an accompanying picture to illustrate each.

When you are finished, tape your paper to the wall. Ask each mom and daughter to do this on her own. When all posters are complete, have everyone introduce herself using her name drawing.

elBOW MatCHarONI

Ask moms and daughters to spread out in the room. Call out things that they may have in common, such as "wears same kind of shoes" or "likes the same kind of food." After calling out each characteristic, individuals rush to find as many people as possible with the same thing in common. Attendees with the same characteristic lock elbows and add people until the leader calls "time" after ten seconds. Disband groups and resume play with a different characteristic. Possible characteristics include birth month, favorite sport, and same middle name.

HUMaN TreaSUre HUNT

Create a list of fifteen to thirty statements to distribute to the moms and daughters in your class. Give the group a period of time to find people who meet the criteria of the different statements on the list. When participants find someone who meets the criteria, they ask that person to sign their list. At the end of the activity, read off the various statements and ask anyone who meets the criteria to stand up. A sample list may include:

- ♥ Has a blue toothbrush
- ♥ Is an only child
- ♥ Hates chocolate
- ♥ Hasn't got all her second teeth
- ♥ Is having a very happy unbirthday today
- ♥ Can stand on her head and count to ten
- ♥ Knows her ABCs backward
- ♥ Has two brothers
- ♥ Has green eyes
- ♥ Had a shower yesterday

getting started with *Building Circles of Grace*

After your class participants have had an opportunity to greet one another, this is a good time to ask moms and daughters to take out their Bibles. Discuss different Bible translations and the benefits of referencing different versions throughout the Bible study. If a passage is difficult to understand in one translation, encourage the girls to try another.

Ask someone to read Psalm 45:11. Take a few minutes so others can share from different Bible translations they may be using. (It may be helpful for the facilitator to bring two or three different translations to class.) The purpose of this exercise is twofold:

- ❤ It demonstrates a helpful strategy during Bible study when a passage is difficult to understand. Check another translation!
- ❤ Psalm 45:11 is a great passage to begin *Building Circles of Grace*. This study is about building Christ-centered relationships. The first chapter discusses the importance of celebrating the beauty within us. God created beauty. The solar system, the earth, and everything within it was designed and created by God—down to the most miniscule details.

preparing for chapter one

Building Circles of Grace leads moms and daughters to discuss what it means to build and sustain Christ-centered relationships beyond their own relationship with Jesus. Some of the toughest experiences we encounter as young girls (and moms, too) are a result of the people we choose as friends. How do you respond with grace to a bully? How do you cope with the loss of a friendship? Can you really make a difference by putting Jesus first when it's not the socially acceptable thing to do? We are going to talk about all these questions and more over the course of this Bible study.

The first week is about learning to celebrate the beauty within us. Beauty means different things to different people. Take a few minutes and ask the girls and moms to share what they think this statement means.

Beauty is in the eye of the beholder.

Do they agree? Ask them to share what they think it means to be beautiful. Listen to their responses, and try to gently include any quiet girls who may not be participating in the discussion.

Celebrating the Beauty of You

Talk with the girls and their moms about how God created each and every one of us. Ask the girls and their moms to turn in their Bibles to the following passage:

> *Before I formed you in the womb I knew you, before you were born I set you apart; I appointed you as a prophet to the nations.*
>
> Jer. 1:5 NIV

Take a few minutes to let the girls read aloud from their different Bible translations. Ask them to share what this Scripture means to them. Reiterate how God created each and every one of us in his image, but he also created each and every thing on the earth to be special and unique. Beauty does not just pertain to girls, but it includes boys. Beauty encompasses all living things and all inanimate things created by God.

NO TWO ALIKE

Take a long roll of butcher paper, and spread it out along the length of the room. Give moms and daughters crayons or markers. Ask them to trace their hands on the paper. Moms trace their daughters' hands and vice versa. Give them time to color and decorate their traced handprint on the butcher paper.

After they are finished, ask for help in taping the length of the paper to the wall. Take a few minutes to compare the handprints and designs. There will be no two alike! Talk about how that is God's design! Each one of us was created by God as an original masterpiece, and he intentionally made us all one of a kind.

This week, remind the girls and their moms to think about beauty through God's eyes. The first chapter of *Building Circles of Grace* is about recognizing that God did not make a mistake when he made us. Think about how special and unique each of us is! Challenge your girls and their moms to celebrate the beauty of themselves and others—not just this week, but every day moving forward.

Thanksgivings and prayer requests

Take the last ten minutes or so of each small group time to share thanksgivings and prayer requests. Give thanks to God for creating each and every one of us with love and detail. Ask God to give us the wisdom and truth to see ourselves and others as he sees us.

These young girls are prayer warriors in training, so keep them in the habit of praying for others and giving thanks when God answers prayers—even if he doesn't answer them the way we thought he would! If resources permit, think of including small notebooks for your class participants, so they may take notes and jot down prayer requests during each meeting. Blessings to you, facilitators! You are planting important seeds of faith. Thank you.

week TWO

Open the class time with prayer. After prayer, welcome everyone and take the first few minutes of class for each person to share one blessing she experienced since the last time you were together as a group.

Follow-Up from Chapter One

Allow some time for mother/daughter teams to share their thoughts and experiences from Chapter One. Some potential questions for discussion:

- ♥ How does our idea of beauty differ from that of God?
- ♥ Is it tough to retrain our brains to see beauty as God defines it rather than by the world's ideals of beautiful? Be real with the girls here and give them a chance to talk about what they think it means to be beautiful. Discuss the dangers of letting the world's perception (or misperception) of beauty dictate our own views.
- ♥ Is beauty on the inside or outside? Discuss the girls' thoughts.
- ♥ Did Chapter One make you think differently about what beauty means? Why or why not?
- ♥ Ask the girls to look up and read two verses: Luke 12:7 and Psalm 139:14. If time permits, allow the girls to share from different Bible translations. What do these Scripture passages mean? Talk about the love and care God took in creating each one of us.
- ♥ Did anyone do the Mom and Me activity from Chapter One? Did they bring portraits to share? How did they like it? How were their pictures similar and/or different?
- ♥ Are we all beautiful? Let them talk through this. God does not make mistakes, and we are all part of God's masterpiece. This could be an opportunity for girls and moms to share their own doubts about how beautiful they really are. Be real, but keep the conversation positive—reinforcing God's reality of beauty always trumps a worldly misperception.

Where Does Your Circle Begin?

After answering any questions about Chapter One, direct the discussion to the topic for Chapter Two. The next chapter is about defining what a relationship is and who makes up our circle of grace. Sometimes we pick the relationships we have, and sometimes we do not get a choice.

Do You Love Your Neighbor?

This game requires no preparation or supplies. Arrange enough chairs in a circle for one less than the number of people in your group. For example, if you have twenty moms and daughters, you'll arrange nineteen seats. Select the mom or daughter who has the next approaching birthday. She'll be the "it" person in the middle of the circle with the primary goal to snag a seat from another mom or daughter.

Here is how that works. Your "it" girl must approach another mom or daughter (hopefully one she doesn't know quite well yet) and introduce herself. Then she will ask her new friend, "Do you love your neighbor?" She can say yes or no. If she says yes, the girls to her left and right must change seats. Your "it" girl has a chance to snag one of them, in the process creating a new "it" girl.

If your girl says no, she must add a condition to her answer. For example, she may say, "No, only if she likes to eat chocolate." Then everyone in the circle who likes chocolate must vacate her seat and quickly find a new one. Conditions can include hair color, ages, etc. Make it fun and give everyone a chance to be the "it" girl.

Forging Friendships—Getting to Know You Box

What you'll need:

- ♥ One small box per person (preferably with lid)
- ♥ Crayons
- ♥ Glue
- ♥ Stickers
- ♥ Markers
- ♥ Craft sticks
- ♥ Scissors
- ♥ Construction paper
- ♥ Magazines

- Give each girl and mom a box with her name on it. Each person will need her own box. For example, if you have ten mother/daughter teams, you will need twenty boxes.
- Talk about how being a friend means getting to know each other first. Explain that everyone has a special box to fill with things to help other girls in Bible study learn more about her.
- Ask each girl and mom to draw a picture of her favorite activity or hobby.
- Ask the girls to draw a picture of their favorite food or cut it out from one of the magazines you have brought.
- Ask the girls to include a creation from paper in her favorite color.
- Each girl can make family puppets with craft sticks and construction paper to represent different members of her family.
- Give the moms and girls a chance to share a few things from their boxes with the group.
- Mention that while there are similarities between people, every girl and mom has something that makes her special and unique. Reinforce the beauty of each individual and encourage the girls to recognize the beauty of others.
- If you run out of time to finish the boxes, ask moms and daughters to finish them at home and bring them back to class the next week.

Friendship Chains

A great way to discuss the concept of friendship is to create a friendship chain. Ask the girls to share qualities that they think make a good friend. They may mention qualities such as honesty, loyalty, and kindness. Give each girl and mom a few strips of construction paper that can be made into a paper chain. Ask the girls and moms to write the names of friends and the qualities that make this person a good friend.

Instruct the girls to create a small friendship chain with their links. After the girls make their own mini-chains, ask them to join their individual friendship chains together to make one long community chain.

Secret Pal Week (Bonus Option)

If moms and girls are keen on the idea, have girls and moms draw names so that each has a secret pal in Bible study. Share the roster and let the girls and their moms know that as secret pals, they may send anonymous notes and cards for their special friends. In a few weeks, we will see if they can guess their secret pals!

Your covenant really comes into play here, especially as your moms and girls commit their time and attendance. Secret pals only work when your small group members attend regularly and engage with one another throughout the length of the study. Otherwise, some girls may not receive secret pal surprises while others do. Talk with your moms if possible before your study begins to get a pulse check on whether this bonus option will be right for you and your small group.

Thanksgivings and prayer requests

Take the last ten minutes or so of the class to share thanksgivings and prayer requests. These young girls are prayer warriors in training, so keep them in the habit of praying for others and giving thanks when God answers prayers—even if he doesn't answer them the way we thought he would!

week Three

Open class time with Prayer. After prayer, welcome everyone and take the first few minutes of class for each person to share one blessing she experienced since the last time you were together as a group.

Follow-Up from Chapter Two

Allow some time for mother/daughter teams to share their thoughts and experiences from Chapter Two. Some potential questions for discussion include:

- ♥ The Holy Trinity can be confusing and difficult to understand. Take time to talk through the Girl of Grace Heart Check questions related to the Trinity. If you sense confusion, there is an optional activity included here to help explain the Trinity is a simple and fun way.
- ♥ What is the difference between an inherited relationship and one you choose for yourself?
- ♥ Can both be a blessing to you?
- ♥ Ruth and Naomi had a special relationship, and it's a beautiful example from the Bible of how familial connections can really bless our lives. Can you share other examples of family relationships like this? (Ask the girls to share examples from their own lives.)
- ♥ Is it important to work on our family relationships as we do the friendships we choose? Why or why not?
- ♥ Ask the girls to read Luke 5:1–11. Talk about how the disciples were an unlikely group of friends, but God brought them together for an extraordinary purpose. Can you think of a time when you made a good friend in an unlikely place or circumstance?
- ♥ Who has a best friend? What makes your BFF your favorite friend?
- ♥ Do we all have the same requirements or preferences for a favored companion? (They'll likely say no.) Why or why not? Talk about how we are all created in God's image, yet we are all created uniquely. We are drawn to different qualities, because we are different people.
- ♥ Ask if anyone remembers the song "O, Be Careful Little Eyes." They

can take a minute to sing the song if they like. Why is this a great guide for us as we develop and maintain friendships?

♥ Was anyone able to have their mother/daughter sleepover? Allow a moment for moms and girls to share.

Optional Activity to Explain the Trinity

Trinity Shamrock
What you will need:

- ♥ Green construction paper
- ♥ A heart template
- ♥ Markers
- ♥ Brads (one small package)
- ♥ Scissors

A little background for your moms and daughters about the shamrock: according to legend, the shamrock was a sacred plant discovered by the Druids of Ireland. These Celtic pagans valued the shamrock for its triad leaf (or three-leaf) formation. The number three was a mystical number in their religion. In the fifth century, St. Patrick, an early Christian missionary, is said to have used the shamrock to teach the doctrine (remember, this is a belief system) of the Holy Trinity to the Irish pagans. The three leaves represent the Father, the Son, and the Holy Spirit. St. Patrick is credited with introducing Christianity to Ireland and converting hundreds of Celtic castles. His clever use of the shamrock to explain the Trinity is what you are going to recreate today!

- ♥ Give each mom and daughter team enough green construction paper to draw three of your heart templates.
- ♥ Using the heart template, ask them to draw and cut out three hearts of equal size. Then have them cut a stem for their shamrock.
- ♥ Ask them to write "God" on one leaf, "Jesus" on the second leaf, and "Holy Spirit" on the third.
- ♥ Assemble the leaves and stems in the shape of a shamrock, and attach the brad to the center so all pieces are secured together.

Encourage the girls to keep their shamrocks with their Bible study supplies as a reminder that the Trinity models perfect community for us.

You've Got a Friend in Me

After answering any questions about Chapter Two, direct the discussion to the topic for Chapter Three. The next chapter addresses a couple of tough topics. We'll talk about what being a friend means to each of us, but the girls will also discuss what happens when we don't stand by a friend when we know we should. What happens when a friend we really like is negatively influencing our ability to make positive choices? What tools does God give us to prepare us for situations like this?

Forging Friendships—Getting to Know You Box

You may have run out of time for moms and daughters to finish their boxes during class last week. Hopefully, each mother/daughter team was able to finish their boxes at home. Remind the girls about the discussion from last week when we talked about how we form new friendships.

Break the moms and daughters into small groups if you have a large class, and ask them to share the contents of their boxes with the group. Take 15 to 20 minutes, and be sure everyone gets a chance to share.

Growing Fruits of the Spirit

Ask your moms and girls to turn in their Bibles to Galatians 5:22–23. Give them a moment to read from various translations they've brought to class. Talk for a moment about how fruit grows.

Now, explain that your mother/daughter teams are going to run in a partner race. Each partnership will represent that we need the Holy Spirit in order to nurture and grow the fruits of our spirit.

Each team will lock arms, and their arms must remain locked through the entire race! Once arms are locked, the facilitator will place a piece of fruit (such as an apple or an orange) on top of the locked elbows. Each team has to make it completely around the track without dropping their fruit. If they drop their fruit, they must go back to the start line.

If elbows come unlocked, that team is out of the game! Even if they drop their fruit, partners must keep their elbows locked as they pick up the fruit and set it back in place to get back in the race. If possible, have a couple of prizes for the top winners.

Gather everyone back in a circle and talk about their experiences during the race. Was it easy to keep elbows in place? Was it easy to carry the fruit? Allow moms and daughters to respond. Then talk about how nurturing and growing the fruit of the Spirit isn't always easy, but we can do it with the help of the Holy Spirit! We can make a choice to partner with the Holy Spirit, who is always present and willing to help.

Fruit of the Spirit Folding Craft Stick Canvas

Explain that this next activity is to help moms and daughters memorize the fruits of the Spirit and serve as a visual reminder to cultivate each characteristic. Once complete, this nifty little tool may be kept in their purse, school bag, or locker—anywhere they will regularly see it and remember why cultivating love, joy, peace, patience, kindness, goodness, faithfulness, gentleness, and self-control are important.

Here's what you'll need:

* Woodsies Mini Jumbo Craft Sticks (10–11 per person)
* Use good quality craft sticks that lay flat.
* The 5/8-inch width works well with 1-inch tape.
* 3M Scotch Masking Tape, 1-inch
* Other brands will work, but this one is recommended. It is the exact color of the craft sticks.
* Permanent markers, crayons, or colored pencils
* Washable markers don't work well because they smear.
* Colored ¼-inch ribbon to tie your folded sticks together when your craft is done.

How to make the canvas:

* Cut the 1-inch masking tape into 4-inch pieces.
* Place two sticks together, side by side, and tape them together, covering both the sticks with the tape.
* Turn the two sticks over so that they are diagonal to you.
* Place another craft stick next to and below the two sticks that you taped together. Use another piece of tape to tape the bottom two sticks together.
* Turn all three sticks over diagonally and place another stick at the bottom of the row and tape the last two sticks together. Keep going until you have a whole row of sticks.
* You can also cover the first and last stick in the row by placing tape over the stick and then folding it back over the stick. It is easier to

write on the tape than the craft stick. The ink soaks into the wood and blurs.

Girls can use permanent markers, pens, or colored pencils to write the Bible verse (Gal. 5:22–23) on the sticks and then decorate them. If someone makes a mistake while working on her canvas, simply pull off the tape where the mistake was made and replace it with new tape.

Tie the finished stacks with colorful ribbon so moms and girls can easily transport their new creations! Encourage them to carry these folding sticks with them as a reminder to cultivate the fruits of their spirits!

Facilitator, if you have time prior to class, make a sample at home to bring with you. It'll help your visual learners! If *you* need a good visual, Google "folding craft stick canvas" to see a finished product or watch a YouTube video showing the process.

Thanksgivings and Prayer requests

Take the last ten minutes or so of the class to share thanksgivings and prayer requests. These young girls are prayer warriors in training, so keep them in the habit of praying for others and giving thanks when God answers prayers— even if he doesn't answer them the way we thought he would!

week Four

OPEN CLaSS time with PRayER. After prayer, welcome everyone and take the first few minutes of class for each person to share one blessing she experienced since the last time you were together as a group.

FOLLOW-UP FROM ChapteR Three

Allow some time for mother/daughter teams to share their thoughts and experiences from Chapter Three. Some potential questions for discussion include:

- ♥ What does it mean to be a favored companion?
- ♥ Read Ecclesiastes 4:9–12. What does the Bible tell us about the importance of friendship in our lives?
- ♥ Can you think of some of the examples of friendship modeled and shared in the Bible? Encourage them to look back in the text of Chapter Three if they need a hint.
- ♥ What is a fair-weather friend?
- ♥ Have any of you had an experience with a fair-weather friend? Would you like to share what happened and how you handled the situation?
- ♥ Can anyone share a time when your friends helped you feel strong in a situation that would have been tough to experience alone?
- ♥ Read Job 2:11–13. Why are friends like Job's rare and special?

Say What?

After answering any questions about Chapter Three, direct the discussion to the topic for Chapter Four. Chapter Four is on the topic of gossip and telling the difference between sharing and gossiping. Take a few minutes to talk with the girls about what it means to gossip. Is it a good thing? Can positive experiences come from gossip? Give them an opportunity to share and discuss. Then lead the mom and daughter teams through the following activities as time permits.

Telephone—a Classic Game That Demonstrates the Dangers of Gossip

Assemble the girls and their moms into a big circle. The classic game of telephone demonstrates just how a story can change as it is passed from one person to the next. Ask one girl or mom to whisper a short phrase into the next person's ear. Then explain that that person will whisper it to the next person and so on until the message has made it completely around the circle. Ask the last person to share the news she heard. Then ask the original whisperer to share what she said. It's likely to be drastically different—especially if you have a large group of participants.

Point out that although it is silly in the game, if you are talking about real people, warped or incomplete stories can be embarrassing or hurtful. Remind the girls about the importance of not repeating a story they hear about someone else unless they know the whole story and have permission to share it.

Take It Back!

Everyone can relate to wishing you could take back something you said, but unfortunately, unwise or unkind words cannot be undone once they are out of your mouth.

Here's what you'll need:

- ♥ Paper plates
- ♥ Travel-sized toothpaste tubes
- ♥ Plastic spoons
- ♥ Plastic knives

Pass out paper plates, toothpaste, and plastic spoons and knives—make sure each mom or daughter gets her own paper plate, toothpaste, etc.

Ask each person to squeeze a large glob of toothpaste on the plate. Give them one minute to try to stuff all the toothpaste back in the tube. When they cannot, explain that gossip is like trying to put the toothpaste back in the tube—you can't really do it and end up with a big mess. This is why it is important to watch your words before they come out of your mouth. Once the words are out, the damage is done and it is difficult to take it back.

IS IT GOSSIP?

Write various statements on small index cards. Make some of them fabricated gossip and the others facts about the mothers and daughters in your group. Assemble everyone into a circle. Explain that you will read a statement to each one and that the person will have to decide if it constitutes fact or gossip. If the person answers correctly, they keep the card. Whoever has the most cards at the end of the game wins a prize.

After reading statements, give the moms and daughters a chance to discuss what is gossiping and what is not. Reiterate how harmful gossiping can be for all parties—that it's hurtful for the person who is at the heart of the juicy discussion, and the person spreading the rumors isn't likely to be viewed positively by others.

GOSSIP Bracelets

Ask the girls and their moms to read James 3:1–12. Talk about how James warns that blessings and curses shouldn't come out of the same mouth. This will be an ongoing activity that will help keep the girls and moms aware of the positive and negative things they say. You can purchase a friendship bracelet kit or assemble the supplies to make friendship bracelets from scratch. These, however, are going to be called "gossip bracelets." Let the moms and daughters work together to make their own bracelets. Everyone should make one.

Challenge your mom and daughter teams to wear their bracelets every day for the next week. When they catch themselves saying something negative, they should switch their gossip bracelet to the other wrist. When they say something affirming, they can move it back. Ask them to try to keep track of how many times they move it in one week.

Thanksgivings and Prayer Requests

Take the last ten minutes or so of the class to share thanksgivings and prayer requests. These young girls are prayer warriors in training, so keep them in the habit of praying for others and giving thanks when God answers prayers— even if he doesn't answer them the way we thought he would!

week Five

open class time with prayer. After prayer, welcome everyone and take the first few minutes of class for each person to share one blessing she experienced since the last time you were together as a group.

Follow-up from Chapter Four

Allow some time for mother/daughter teams to share their thoughts and experiences from Chapter Four. Some potential questions for discussion include:

- What is the difference between sharing and gossiping?
- Why can gossip hurt your circle of grace?
- Read Proverbs 16:28. Ask the girls to explain what the passage means.
- Can you use your words to share words of affirmation to your friends and other people?
- What are the differences between the effects of gossip and the effects of words of affirmation?
- Can you use words of affirmation to lift up people outside your own circle? How?
- Does anyone want to share her experiences from the Mom and Me activity this week? Give the girls and their moms a few minutes to share.

i Will if you Will!

After answering any questions about Chapter Four, direct the discussion to the topic for Chapter Five. Chapter Five is about peer pressure. Talk with the girls about what peer pressure means. Can you have positive and negative forms of peer pressure? Give them an opportunity to share and discuss. Then lead the mom and daughter teams through the following activities as time permits.

HONEY, I LOVE YOU

Give the girls a chance to experience peer pressure in a lighthearted setting. This is a game where the girls and their moms must resist smiling or laughing, even with their friends. Ask your mom and daughter teams to form a circle, with one girl in the middle who asks anyone else as comically as possible, "Honey, do you love me?" The person asked must answer, "Honey, I love you, but I just can't smile." If she laughs or smiles, she becomes the next "It."

STANDING AGAINST PEER PRESSURE

Materials needed:

- ♥ Balloons (enough for one per mother/daughter team)
- ♥ Black permanent marker
- ♥ Empty water bottles (enough for one per mother/daughter team)

Ask the moms to blow up their balloon and draw a face on it with a permanent marker. Allow the ink to dry, and then instruct moms to deflate the balloons. Now, show moms and daughters how to insert their balloons into the empty water bottles and pull the opening of the balloon over the mouth of the bottle. The balloon should be hanging inside the bottle.

Ask the girls if they can blow up the balloon. Give them an opportunity to try blowing up their balloons in the bottles. Tell them to blow hard into the balloon so that it will inflate. No matter how hard they blow, the balloon will not inflate inside the bottle. This gives us a picture of what it's like to be influenced by negative peer pressure. Peers are the people around us—friends and family. And pressure is when we feel forced to be and act a certain way.

Explain that the balloon represents a person and the bottle is peer pressure. No matter how hard she tries, when she allows herself to be surrounded by negative peer pressure—people trying to influence her to act in a certain way—she is not able to grow into the person God intended. It stifles her. It chokes her. It keeps her from growing spiritually.

Now ask moms to remove the balloons from the bottles and ask them to blow their balloons up. The face they drew on the balloon will appear. When this person freed herself from peer pressure, when she decided it wasn't important to please others who wanted to force her to live and believe a certain way—she was free to grow and thrive and become what God intended.

Ask the girls and their moms to turn to Romans 12:2 in their Bibles. Let them share their thoughts and experiences about the exercise and what God shares in this passage about peer pressure.

role-playing activity

Put together several different scenarios prior to your class. Divide the girls and their moms into two groups. It's fun to put the moms in one group and the girls in another. Give the groups time to "practice" their scenarios, and then let them perform in front of one another.

Leave a ". . ." at the end of each scenario so each group has to come up with their own way to address the peer pressure situation. After each group performs, take a few minutes for them to share why they chose to handle their scenario the way they did. See the Free Resources section at the end of this study for sample scenarios to use during this activity. Some groups prefer to use the sample scenarios, and then allow the girls to get creative and make up their own. Be flexible and allow the girls to role-play organically if possible. Meaningful and relevant discussions have blossomed from these activities during the pilot groups about situations some girls were actively living out in their day-to-day lives. The strategies that were brainstormed became tools these girls were able to take away and apply immediately.

Thanksgivings and prayer requests

Take the last ten minutes or so of the class to share thanksgivings and prayer requests. These young girls are prayer warriors in training, so keep them in the habit of praying for others and giving thanks when God answers prayers—even if he doesn't answer them the way we thought he would!

week six

Open class time with prayer. After prayer, welcome everyone and take the first few minutes of class for each person to share one blessing she experienced since the last time you were together as a group.

Follow-up from chapter five

Allow some time for mother/daughter teams to share their thoughts and experiences from Chapter Five. Some potential questions for discussion include:

- ♥ Remind me what peer pressure is. Can anyone share an example?
- ♥ Is peer pressure negative or positive? (The girls should tell you it is both.)
- ♥ What are some positive ways you can influence others?
- ♥ Read 1 Corinthians 15:33. Ask the girls to explain what the passage means.
- ♥ Ask the girls to brainstorm ways they can positively influence people who encourage them to make bad choices.
- ♥ Does anyone want to share her experiences from the Mom and Me activity this week? Give the girls and their moms a few minutes to share.

No one likes a bully

After answering any questions about Chapter Five, direct the discussion to the topic for Chapter Six. Chapter Six is on the topic of bullying. Give the mother/daughter teams a chance to discuss what bullying looks like to them. Then lead the teams through the following activities as time permits.

Wrinkled Wendy

Activity adapted and printed with permission and special thanks from James Burns and The Bully Proof Classroom. http://bullyproofclassroom.com /great-anti-bullying-activities.

On a big tablet or rolled butcher paper, ask each mom and daughter team to trace an outline of a full-body person on their paper. Once the outline has been traced, give each mom and daughter a chance to write unkind, rude, and disrespectful statements all over their outlines. These are statements that could be made to another person, such as, "You're a loser," "Nobody likes you," or "You are dumb." Identify the drawing as a girl named Wendy. After Wendy is completely filled with a variety of negative comments, have each team crumple their drawing and then un-crumple it. Hang the wrinkled drawings around the room. Explain to the group that these drawings are examples of what negative comments can do to a person who is bullied. Bullying comments can destroy a person's self-image and often lead to a defeated body language in the victim. Give the girls a chance to view all the Wrinkled Wendys.

Lead the girls in a discussion as they observe how the paper can be smoothed out, but creases from the wrinkles still remain. Words can cut deeply and leave scars on our hearts. Give moms and daughters a few minutes to share with one another about negative words that have left wrinkles on their hearts. After a few minutes, bring everyone together again.

Next ask the mom and daughter teams to do the drawing again. This time, they should write as many positive comments on the drawing as possible. Statements like, "You did such a nice job," or "I enjoy your friendship." Fill it with really nice statements. Being careful not to wrinkle these outlines, post them around the room. The new outline is now just called Wendy. What is the difference between Wrinkled Wendy and Wendy? Give the moms and girls a chance to discuss.

THE COOL CrOWD

Begin with every mom and daughter receiving a playing card, facedown.
Explain the following:

- ♥ You are to not look at your card or tell anyone else what her card is.
- ♥ Each person should place the card on her forehead (or walk showing the card, but not looking at their own card!) with the face of the card facing away from her head.
- ♥ Begin to mingle with each other, but treat everyone based on the "face value" of her card. For example, low cards (2–5) won't get much attention or are avoided; midrange cards (6–10) are treated with respect but not overly so; royal cards (J, Q, K, A) are the best of the

deck—those cards are the ones you try to hang out with, treat well, and think are really cool.

Allow the moms and daughters to mingle for several minutes, treating others based on face value. After a few minutes, ask them to divide into groups based on how they have been treated—low cards, midrange, and royalty. Talk with the girls and their moms about how it doesn't take very long to figure out what group you belong to based on how people treat you.

Ask members from each group why they felt like they belonged in that group and how people made them feel. Ask the girls if they remember talking about the Golden Rule. Give them a chance to remember and discuss what this is. Ask the girls how it applies to their lives—meaning we should treat others as royalty, not low cards, even if that's how others treat them.

Have everyone take the cards off their foreheads and check to see if they are correct in guessing which level card they have. After this activity, you can easily lead into a bullying discussion where you identify and define what bullying is, types of bullying, why people bully, what to do if you see bullying or are bullied, and how to avoid becoming a bully yourself.

At the end, remind the girls that bullying stops with them. It has to be a personal and individual choice to make it stop and to treat all those around them as if they were all royalty.

MaKe IT a CHaIN reaCTION!

Bring back the chain you made as a class when discussing Chapter Two. Remind the girls that the chain is comprised of characteristics that make a good friend. This week, you are going to add to your chain by adding characteristics that help stop the acts and impact of bullying.

Give the girls and their moms time to discuss possible characteristics with one another. Then give each girl and mom a few strips of construction paper that can be made into a paper chain. After each team has brainstormed a few characteristics, ask the girls to add their links to the bigger chain from Chapter Two. Give them a chance to share their links as a group.

Thanksgivings and Prayer requests

Take the last ten minutes or so of the class to share thanksgivings and prayer requests. These young girls are prayer warriors in training, so keep them in the habit of praying for others and giving thanks when God answers prayers—even if he doesn't answer them the way we thought he would!

Week Seven

Open the class time with prayer. After prayer, welcome everyone and take the first few minutes of class for each person to share one blessing she experienced since the last time you were together as a group.

Follow-Up from Chapter Six

Allow some time for mother/daughter teams to share their thoughts and experiences from Chapter Six. Some potential questions for discussion include:

- ♥ What is a bully? Can anyone give me an example from the Bible? (Let the girls brainstorm and share.)
- ♥ Can you think of reasons that motivate a person to be mean to others?
- ♥ Have any of you ever been a bully? (Take a moment to talk with the girls about how we all show meanness from time to time. Let them talk about what they are feeling when they are mean to others. Then ask them if thinking about what makes us act out helps us understand our bully a little better.
- ♥ How do you respond when someone is mean to you? Let the girls brainstorm and discuss.
- ♥ Read Matthew 5:43–48. Ask the girls to explain what the passage means.
- ♥ How can praying and living out Matthew 5:43–48 be life-changing—for ourselves as well as the people we interact with?
- ♥ Does anyone want to share their experience with the Mom and Me activity? How did it feel to write a letter to a mean girl who has hurt you? Did you deliver the letter? (Give the girls a chance to talk about the experience, and encourage those who didn't do this activity to make time for it over the next week or so.)
- ♥ What are some ways you can make a positive difference when you encounter a situation where someone else is being bullied?

social vs. "un"social media

After answering any questions about Chapter Six, direct the discussion to the topic for Chapter Seven. In Chapter Seven, we will discuss the effect of virtual connectivity. What is social media? Is it positive or negative? What impact does social media have on our circles of grace? Then lead the mom and daughter teams through the following activities as time permits.

Jam relay

You'll need the following:

- ♥ Jar of jam
- ♥ Spoons
- ♥ Small plastic bowls

Place jam in bowls on a table on one side of the room. Split moms and daughters into teams (perhaps mamas against daughters). The idea is for each team to get their jam from one end of the room to another in the shortest amount of time. The catch? They can only use their hands! They may not use the bowl or the spoon. The first team to relay their jam to the opposite side of the room wins.

After girls have a chance to clean their hands, discuss:

- ♥ What would have happened if they had not cleaned their hands? The jam is sticky and leaves our hands feeling that way, too.
- ♥ If we were to touch other things with our sticky hands, we would leave sticky fingerprints on everything we touched.
- ♥ This is how social media works. Everything we post—our words, pictures, videos—sticks with us into our future and can affect our future selves' school, employment, friendships, and so on.

Social media vs. unsocial media

You'll need the following:

- ♥ Pieces of paper
- ♥ Pencils

Give each mom and daughter team a piece of paper, and ask them to draw a line down the middle of the paper. On one side, ask them to write a heading titled "The Good," and on the other side, ask them to write "The Bad." Give your teams time to discuss and list what they think are pros and cons of social media.

Come back as a group and discuss together.

Thanksgivings and prayer requests

Take the last ten minutes or so of the class to share thanksgivings and prayer requests. These young girls are prayer warriors in training, so keep them in the habit of praying for others and giving thanks when God answers prayers—even if he doesn't answer them the way we thought he would!

week eight

OPEN the ClaSS time With Prayer. After prayer, welcome everyone and take the first few minutes of class for each person to share one blessing she experienced since the last time you were together as a group.

FOllOW-UP From Chapter Seven

Allow some time for mother/daughter teams to share their thoughts and experiences from Chapter Seven. Some potential questions for discussion include:

- ♥ What is social media? Take a moment to ask the moms and daughters in your group which social media sites they utilize. (Care should be used so that girls who do not yet have permission to use social media sites do not feel excluded. This topic is still extremely relevant for them, and much fruit can still be borne through discussion. This is information these girls will be able to apply when the time comes for them to engage in social media outlets.)
- ♥ How much time do we spend perusing these outlets each day?
- ♥ What *need* does social media meet within us? Give moms and daughters a chance to share.
- ♥ Does the content you view on social media affect the way you see yourself or view others?
- ♥ Read Luke 11:34. Ask the girls to explain why they think it may or may not be important to guard their hearts while using apps like Facebook, Instagram, or Twitter.
- ♥ Is there a difference between being connected and connectedness? If yes, describe it.
- ♥ Do you value social media interactions more than real-life relationships? Why or why not?
- ♥ Do you give as much time to God as you do to electronic devices and social media?

Developing accountability

After answering any questions about Chapter Seven, direct the discussion to the topic for Chapter Eight. Chapter Eight is about sustaining your circle of grace and what it means to develop accountability. Take time to discuss how God holds us accountable today. Who else holds us accountable for our actions and choices? Why is it important for us to be held accountable? Let the girls and moms share their thoughts and discuss. Then, lead the mom and daughter teams through the following activities as time permits.

BUILDING encouragers

Before class, tape or mark off three- to four-foot squares on the floor (depending on the space in your meeting room). Masking tape works well and is easy to remove later.

Break your moms and daughters into teams of four to six. Using the verse from the Mom and Me activity in Chapter Eight, print or write each word from Hebrews on separate index cards. Each team will need their own set of index cards reflecting the whole Bible verse. If you have several groups, it may be helpful to use colored index cards so each team has an assigned color during the game.

> *Let us hold tightly without wavering to the hope we affirm, for God can be trusted to keep his promise. Let us think of ways to motivate one another to acts of love and good works. And let us not neglect our meeting together, as some people do, but encourage one another, especially now that the day of his return is drawing near.*
>
> Heb. 10:23–25 NLT

Explain to the moms and daughters that the squares are "home base." The object of the game is to collect all the cards of the Bible verse and put them in the correct order. The trick is that each set of index cards is scattered haphazardly outside of the circle and well out of arm's reach. In order to collect the cards, teams will have to work together to gather them! Someone must remain on "home base" at all times, and all team members must remain connected to one another as they work together to collect the cards and assemble their verses.

Each team will begin the game standing inside their "home base." It may be helpful to have the Bible verse referenced on a poster board or bulletin board before you begin. At the very least, ask moms and daughters to open their Bibles and locate the verse before the game begins. Read through the verse together so everyone is familiar with the order in which the index cards will need to go.

Start the timer, and let the teams go! The first team to collect their index cards without breaking their human chain and assembling their Bible verse in the correct order wins the game. If time, switch up the teams (moms vs. daughters).

Afterward, discuss:

♥ Would it have been possible for one person to gather all the cards without leaving home base?
♥ Look at Hebrews 10:23–25 again. Why do you think God calls us to be encouragers?
♥ What does encouragement have to do with accountability?

ACCOUNTABILITY BALLOON GAME

The purpose of this game is to demonstrate that holding someone else accountable is not an easy task. It requires presence, patience, and encouragement.

For this game, you will need:

♥ A balloon for each mother/daughter team
♥ A trash bag or grocery sack for each mother/daughter team

Give each mom and daughter a blown-up balloon. The object of the game is to carry the balloon together without using their hands or arms. Moms and daughters may use their shoulders, hips, legs, or whatever else as long as they are not using their hands or arms to touch, balance, or carry the balloon.

Use masking tape or crepe paper to mark the "start line," and ask your teams to line up along the line with their balloons on the floor in front of them. On your mark, mom and daughter teams will pick up their balloon (without using their hands or arms) and race to the other side of the room as fast as they can go without dropping their balloon. Once they reach the other side, they will work together to get their balloon into the sack or bag. If a team drops their balloon, they must go back to the start line and begin again. The first team to reach their sack and successfully deposit their balloon wins the round! If time permits, play a few more rounds.

BIBLE STUDY MEMENTO

Take time for a group photo. Your last class is a great time to let the girls make a picture frame, ornament, or some other type of craft where you can add a photo. Let the girls decorate their own craft of your choice. Encourage the girls and moms to sign each other's crafts as a special memento from your time together.

Thanksgivings and Prayer Requests

Spend the last few minutes of class taking prayer requests and giving thanks that God brought your group together. His plan is perfect, and you are all part of that grand design! Before you go, close in prayer.

Free resources

Sample Bible Study Covenant

Attendance

We commit to arriving on time so as not to disrupt the group process.

The group sessions will begin at 6:30 P.M. and end by 8:00 P.M.

We will begin to gather at 6:15 P.M., but study sessions will begin promptly at 6:30 P.M.

If we cannot attend a class, we will contact one of the facilitators or another class member before the class begins so the class knows we will not be there.

Preparation

We will do the reading and reflections assigned in each lesson as a basis for contributing to the group discussion.

Respect

We will respect one another, accepting what each one shares of herself and not monopolizing time and discussions. We will turn cell phones off or use the vibrate setting if we must have them on for emergencies.

Confidentiality

We will value what is experienced and shared within the group as a treasure entrusted to us for safekeeping. We will not break the confidence entrusted to us by others.

Prayer

We will commit to praying for one another by name.

Sample role-playing scenarios for peer pressure

Scenario a – The Divorce

CHaracters:

Mary – a girl whose parents are going through a messy, public divorce

Bethany – a friend of Mary's who has not spent a lot of time with her recently

Several other girls who are classmates of Mary and Bethany's at school

Setting:

Outside the school building before or after school or in the cafeteria during lunch

Action:

- Bethany and several girls are standing together discussing their favorite music star—a hot debate between Justin Bieber and One Direction.
- Mary walks past.
- The girls stop talking to stare at Mary as she walks by, but they make no attempt to speak with her or invite her to join their discussion.
- Mary clearly notices the girls' stares and tries to walk by with her head down.
- Bethany wants to say hi, but she is afraid of what her other friends may think.
- The girls (except Bethany) quickly begin whispering before Mary is completely past them about what "everyone is saying" about Mary's dad. The rumor is he made some pretty bad choices and now Mary's parents are going through a messy and cruel divorce.
- Bethany remains silent.
- Mary has never been popular and generally keeps to herself, but now she seems "even more weird."
- Mary walks away.

What form is peer pressure taking in this scenario? What other behaviors do you notice? Who feels pressured? How could this scenario have played out differently?

Scenario B – The Game

Characters:

Jessica – a girl who is not very good at sports and is generally picked last for everything at school

Tabitha – the sports star

Several other classmates who are pretty talented athletes and generally thought of as popular kids

Laura – A classmate who is well liked and is not usually seen taunting or picking on other kids

Setting:

In the locker room after gym class at school

Action:

- ♥ Tabitha and her classmates (not including Jessica) are grumbling about the PE coach and how she made them run extra laps for picking on Jessica during and after today's PE game.
- ♥ Jessica was picked last—AGAIN—and the team that finally got stuck with her lost. It happens that Tabitha was team captain that day and made no secret that Jessica was the reason they lost.
- ♥ Even though Jessica wasn't the only player on the team, the other teammates join Tabitha in blaming her for the crushing loss and haven't let her hear the end of it.
- ♥ After they picked on Jessica during gym class, the PE coach punished the classmates by making them run laps while the rest of class was able to begin getting dressed for their next class.
- ♥ After the coach goes into her office, Tabitha and her teammates push Jessica into the lockers and tell her she is such a loser.
- ♥ Jessica bows her head and sinks onto a bench alone.

- Tabitha and her classmates walk away laughing and throwing awful looks toward Jessica.
- Laura, who was on the opposing team that day, watched the whole scene from the end of the row of lockers.

What form is peer pressure taking in this scenario? What other behaviors do you notice? Who feels pressured? How could this scenario have played out differently?

Scenario C – Sneaky Girls

Characters:

Lori – a popular girl who often changes clothes when she gets to school because her mom won't let her wear what she really wants

Nancy – a new friend of Lori's who really wants to fit in to the popular crowd

A group of girls from the popular crowd at school

Setting:

At Lori's house for a slumber party in celebration of Lori's birthday

Action:

- Lori, Nancy, and the girls are talking and laughing in Lori's room after Lori's parents have finally gone to bed.
- One of the girls digs into her bag to show the group the makeup she borrowed from her older sister (a senior in high school) without asking.
- Nancy was so excited to get an invitation, but she's realized tonight that she has hardly anything in common with these girls.
- Lori has been playing music that Nancy is forbidden to hear, and the movie they watched at the party was PG-13. Even though Nancy's parents sometimes allow her to watch PG-13 movies, she's pretty sure the one they watched tonight would not have been approved.
- Now Nancy is realizing that one of the girls she has admired and secretly envied is not the person she thought. The girls have been talking about how to get away with wearing makeup at school, and

one of the girls snuck makeup from her older sister so the girls can practice tonight.

- ♥ Lori and the other girls excitedly dig into the makeup bag, trying to decide what to try on first.
- ♥ Nancy silently watches from her spot on the floor.

What form is peer pressure taking in this scenario? What other behaviors do you notice? Who feels pressured? How could this scenario have played out differently?

ABOUT THE AUTHOR

Catherine Bird is an author, speaker, and Bible teacher who is passionate about moms and tween girls and loves to encourage each—small and tall—in their own journey of faith. She and her husband, Travis, are proud parents to two beautiful girls. As a mom of two daughters, Catherine understands how unique the mother/daughter bond truly is. The hunger to strengthen this bond and develop a deeper relationship with Christ is what led Catherine to prayerfully pursue ministry with moms and tween girls.

Catherine is the author of the Girls of Grace Bible study series, which currently includes: *Becoming a Girl of Grace: A Bible Study for Tween Girls and Their Moms* and *Building Circles of Grace, A Girl of Grace Study.* Through Bible study, Catherine seeks to help mothers and tween daughters discover God's truth in a new and engaging way, reinforcing how incredibly applicable the Bible is for their lives today.

Catherine and her family currently live near Austin, Texas, with one loyal Australian Shepherd and the quirkiest chocolate Labrador Retriever ever. When Catherine is not at her desk writing, she can often be found in yoga class, scoping out some fun new hiking destination with her family, or jumping on the trampoline with her girls. She also believes wholeheartedly in yoga pants, Taco Tuesday, and Texas Aggie football. Catherine holds a bachelor's degree from Texas A&M University.

NOTES